"This clear, concise, and consistent presentation is a valuable resource for the entire religious community. Those who read each verse of the Bible in a literal fashion will be challenged to think beyond what others have told them it means. Those that know that the Bible has much to offer, but who have trouble accepting its teachings in the light of their own experience, will feel empowered to look for the Truth, which is sometimes veiled by timebound language, metaphor, and illustration. In particular, lesbians and gays 'who believe in a good God, who reverence the Bible, and who also want to believe in themselves,' to whom the author dedicates his work, will find a very Friendly invitation to continue their faith journey with the Bible as an affirming companion along the way."

Lyle Jenks
Friends Journal, April 1995

Among the Millennium Edition updates:

... Luke and Matthew in the gospels speak of the Centurion and his slave boy that Jesus healed. Analysis of the translations shows that the slave boy was doubtlessly the Centurion's same-sex lover, yet neither Jesus, Matthew nor Luke casts any negative judgment on this.

... New research uncovers a broad awareness of female same-sex love in the ancient world.

... Original and novel research suggests that David not only had a loving sexual liaison with Jonathan, but also may have had a sexual liaison with Jonathan's father, King Saul, and this was a cause of jealousy between father and son.

What the Bible *Really* Says about Homosexuality

*T*he law of the Lord is perfect, reviving the
    soul;
    the decrees of the Lord are sure, making
    wise the simple;
the precepts of the Lord are right, rejoicing the heart;
the commandment of the Lord is clear, enlightening
    the eyes;
the fear of the Lord is pure, enduring forever;
the ordinances of the Lord are true and righteous
    altogether.
More to be desired are they than gold, even much
    fine gold;
sweeter also than honey, and dripping of the honey-
    comb.

What the **Bible** *Really* Says about Homosexuality

Millennium Edition
Updated and Expanded

Daniel A. Helminiak, Ph.D.

ALAMO SQUARE PRESS
New Mexico

What the Bible *Really* Says About Homosexuality (Millennium Edition)
©2000 by Daniel A. Helminiak, Ph.D.

First Printing, April 2000
Second Printing, April 2001
Third Printing, April 2002
Fourth Printing, April 2003
Fifth Printing, April 2004
Sixth Printing, April 2005
Seventh Printing, April 2006
Eighth Printing, September 2007
Ninth Printing, October 2008
Tenth Printing, April 2010
Eleventh Printing, November 2011
Twelfth Printing, February 2014

What the Bible *Really* Says About Homosexuality
© 1994 by Daniel A. Helminiak, Ph.D.

First Printing, May 1994
Second Printing, October 1994
Third Printing, March 1995
Fourth Printing, August 1996
Fifth Printing, April 1997
Sixth Printing, May 1998
Seventh Printing, August 1999

Library of Congress Catalog Card Number: 94-070336

ISBN: 1-886360-09-X

13   12

To lesbian women and gay men
who believe in a good God and reverence the Bible
and who also want to be able to believe in themselves

Table of Contents

*L*et us therefore no longer pass judgment on
one another,
but resolve instead never to put a stumbling
block or hindrance in the way of another.
I know and am persuaded in the Lord Jesus that
nothing is unclean in itself;
but it is unclean for anyone who thinks it unclean.

Romans 14:13-14

Foreword

There is no book I love more nor one that has shaped my life more dramatically than the Bible. Yet, had I not escaped the literalism of my Christian fundamentalist upbringing, I could not make that statement, for long before now I would have either dismissed the Bible as a hopelessly ignorant and prejudiced ancient religious document or I would have denied reality and become myself a small-minded religious bigot, using literal scriptures to justify my prejudices. A literal Bible, in my opinion, admits no other options.

In my priestly and episcopal career I have watched the literal Bible be quoted to justify racial segregation, to ensure the continued sexist oppression of women by the Christian church, and to perpetuate a killing homophobia in our corporate life.

Had I lived in an earlier part of history, I would have seen the Bible quoted to condemn Copernicus, who asserted that the sun did not occupy the center of the universe, and Galileo, who said that the sun did not rotate around the earth. I would have seen the insights of Isaac Newton challenged by a biblical view of God that could only be described as supernatural magic. I would have witnessed the church's attack upon Charles Darwin in the name of a brand of creationism that today is totally dismissed. Perhaps worst of all, I would have watched while religious people appealed to the literal text of the Bible to support the most inhumane treatment of fellow human beings—the institution of slavery.

11

In this volume, Daniel A. Helminiak, a Roman Catholic priest, brilliantly and courageously explores the biblical texts which are today used to condemn, oppress and marginalize God's children who are gay and lesbian. He brings to his scriptural analysis the heart of a Christian pastor who has stood beside the victims of a virulent prejudice. He goes beyond the literal words of the text to enter into the spirit of the Bible, where he confronts a God who created us all in the divine image, a Christ who values each of us infinitely and a Holy Spirit who calls us into the fullness of our humanity. He dares to set aside the culturally conditioned biblical words for the power of his Lord, who embraced the outcasts of his society whether they were lepers, Samaritans or those who were thought to be possessed by demonic spirits.

Father Helminiak's words will bring hope to many who feel that God has rejected them, and his book will help to make the church aware that it cannot claim to be the body of Christ if it fails to welcome all whom Christ would welcome. His work will also engender hostility, maybe even in official church circles. That is always the way it is when prejudices are challenged, even the prejudices of those who claim to speak for God.

I welcome his work and commend it to all who seek to know both the heart of Christ and the work of God that sometimes works unseen and unrecognized beneath the words of scripture.

The Right Reverend John S. Spong;
Bishop, The Diocese of Newark
The Episcopal Church

Preface to Millennium Edition

Since the first edition of this book appeared in 1994, over 50 thousand copies have been printed. The book has sold consistently over the years. Its goal was to make available in easily readable form a summary of a growing body of scholarly literature on homosexuality in the Bible. Even in 1994, the inevitable conclusion of the scholarly research was already clear. Taken on its own terms and in its own time, the Bible nowhere condemns homosexuality as we know it today.

In the meantime, scholars have continued their research, and some exciting new insights have emerged. That original conclusion holds as solid as ever. It gets ever more certain. At this point in time, it should be considered outrageous for any educated person to quote the Bible to condemn homosexuality. At the very least, the meaning of the relevant texts is so disputed that, in fairness and honesty, no one can use them that way. But even more that this, as this book shows, the fact is that the Bible offers no condemnation pertinent to today's discussion.

This book has been a blessing and a surprising success. On several occasions people confided to me that it saved them from suicide, and many others, that it resurrected for them a long buried religious commitment. In addition, it has become a standard reference on homosexuality in the Bible. So this book needs to be fully credible and up-to-date. Hence, this new edition.

It is appropriate that its publication coincide with the turn of the millennium. Hopefully, this book will contribute to a broadened awareness that will leave the literalist Bible out of the discussion about lesbian and gay relationships. Hopefully, also in other ways personal preferences and religious opinions will graciously give way to tolerance, compassion and delight in commonalities. Then hopefully, the global society of the third millennium will be truly an era of peace, an era of understanding, acceptance and justice for all.

There are four important changes in this new edition. First, there is a new section on Jesus and what seems to be his encounter with a gay man. There is also new material on King Saul's possible sexual relationship with David. Second, there is a new presentation on the "abomination" of Leviticus 18 and 20. The latest research shows that this prohibition is very limited, indeed, and that ancient Jewish religion was tolerant of a range of sexual practices. In fact, a notion of homo- or heterosexuality was not even a consideration; it is a foreign concept in ancient Israel. Third, the milestone work of Bernadette Brooten influences this edition in many places. Brooten's book, *Love Between Women*, stands with John Boswell's and L. William Countryman's as turning points in the scholarly discussion. She researched lesbianism in the ancient world and showed, among other things, that contrary to the standard line, there is much to be known on the subject. This book includes explicit treatment of Brooten in the discussion of Romans, on which she focused her biblical research. She presented a new and challenging interpretation of Paul's teaching about the "unnatural," which I have taken into account. Fourth, I refocused the chapter on 1 Corinthians and 1 Timothy as I become more and more uncertain that *arsenokoitai* refers specifically to male-male sex at all. Reversing my earlier and perhaps overly careful opinion, I begin to believe that in their general conclusion Boswell and Countryman were right about *arsenokoitai*.

In addition, in response to critics of the first edition, in a number of places I have also provided more detailed biblical references. As a result, there are more chapter-and-verse citations in this new edition. Of course, I updated the list of Sources, but as in the first edition, I left the list in chronological, not alphabetical order, so that reading through it could supply something of a history of the scholarship on this question. I also added an explicit outline to the chapter on Romans so that the argument of this long and most important chapter is clear. And I edited the whole book to bring it up to date and to correct minor errors and ambiguities.

As in the first writing, in mind and conscience I struggled with the research as I reworked this book. Again I can say that I have written here what I believe to be the most solidly supported conclusions. People may differ with them, but no one can say they are arbitrary or biased. My intent is to help free people for honest and wholesome living, and such a thing can rest only on the truth, as best we can determine it. In preparing this revision, I have done my best.

I am deeply indebted to Thomas Hanks of the international ministry *Other Sheep* and also to Bruce Jarstfer and Richard Woods for their generous pointers to recent scholarship that needed to be included in this revised edition. Besides those listed in the Preface to the first edition, whom I thank again, for help in this new edition I also extend thanks to John Adamski, Terry Bird and Clark Lemonds, Kerry Clark, Raymond Machesney, Pat Mcarron and Sean Monroe. Of course, the final responsibility for what is written here rests with me. May this writing contribute to building a world worthy of God and thus also worthy of us all.

Preface to First Edition

Since 1977, in Boston, San Antonio and Austin, I have ministered as a Roman Catholic priest to the lesbian and gay community—mostly through Dignity. Dignity is a support group for lesbian, gay and bisexual Catholics and their friends.

I have come to know the gay community probably as well as anybody, and I have become aware of too many horrors:

- Thirty to 40 percent of the youth living on the streets are teenagers who were thrown out or left their homes because they are homosexual.

- Thirty percent of teenage suicides are among homosexual youth. Proportionately, this figure is at least three to four times higher than for other adolescents. [A 1997 study in Massachusetts found the rate of attempted suicides six times higher.]

- People lose their jobs because their boss does not like "queers."

- Parents lose custody of their children or visitation rights for being lesbian or gay.

- Men and women are evicted from their apartments or their houses are burned—because somebody said they were gay.

- Gay men and lesbians are routinely beaten up—and murdered—for being homosexual.

• Public officials make abusive comments about the homosexual minority and easily get away with it.

• A judge hands down a blatantly prejudiced judgment against a gay man's murderers and then is easily reelected.

• A presidential administration and much of the nation ignore an epidemic that in the USA was initially most prevalent among homosexual men.

• A gay man dies of AIDS in his home, locked away from every outsider, without any medical attention, because his family did not want others to know.

• Much human potential is squashed and wasted in people who live for years in secret self-hatred, taught to be afraid of their own hearts.

And there is more, so much more, that most people never know. The standard media are selective in the news they report. Prejudice, downright loathing for homosexuals, is condoned in our society. All this I have come to know too well over the years.

Living in the Bible Belt since 1981, I came to another sad realization: Bible religion plays a major role in allowing those horrors to happen. Quote the Bible, and all discussion suddenly comes to an end. Supposedly, the Bible condemns homosexuality, and some people take that to mean that the Bible justifies hatred and cruelty against gays and lesbians.

Of course, bigotry will have its day, and it will claim to have God on its side—against Jews, against Muslims, against Blacks, against women, against gays. Thus has it always been.

But more reasoned voices also emerge from within religion. Recent research on the Bible shows that, at the very least, the same-sex acts that are the focus of biblical concern were not what we mean by "homosexuality" today. The Bible conceived of the matter very differently in a very different world. Even more, this research shows that the Bible is basically indifferent to homosexuality in itself. The Bible is concerned, as with heterosexuality, only when practices violate other moral requirements.

18

This information needs to be shared. Lesbian and gay people, condemned on the basis of Bible quotes, need to be able to respond intelligently, knowing they are not rejecting God's word. People raised in a strict Bible tradition, struggling with the literal text, need to be able, in good conscience, to find compassionate teaching on homosexuality in the Bible. People who choose to follow the "literal reading" of the Bible need to understand how others, in good faith, can insist the Bible does not condemn homosexuality.

So I present this little book. My commitment to the common good compels me. My goal is to make current information available to people who simply cannot plow through scholarly tomes. My hope is to help diffuse the power of unthinking religion and prejudice and to foster a world that is more compassionate, loving and just.

This book is a popular presentation. I have written as simply as I am able. I do not cite all the historical evidence nor repeat all the intricate discussions. Without completely ignoring the important differences of opinion, I present just one consistent position.

I have agonized over parts of this text. If the conclusion comes down squarely on one side of the question, that is because I honestly believe the evidence falls that way. To be sure, this is not a position that everyone will welcome. Those who can show reason to read the evidence differently must certainly draw another conclusion. But all must at least admit that this book reports some of the best scholarly opinion of our day.

As a Roman Catholic—and more importantly, a thinking person—I do not presume the Bible provides the last word on sexual ethics. In my mind, the matter is more complicated than that. Historical, cultural, philosophical, psychological, sociological, medical, spiritual and personal factors all come to bear on the matter. Nonetheless, biblical teaching is an important basis for any Judeo-Christian belief. And every opinion, religious or otherwise, should rest on facts.

To me this seems to be fact: the Bible supplies no real basis for the condemnation of homosexuality.

Therefore, people must stop opposing homosexuality merely by quoting the Bible, because, taken on its own terms, the Bible simply does not support their case. If they have some other reason for their opposition, they ought to get clear what that reason is and state it up front.

That is the challenge I pose with this book—for those who oppose homosexuality. For those who are homosexual or who support those who are, I offer this book as some consolation: the Bible is not against them. For those who are somewhere in the middle, not knowing where to stand, I hope this book will help them make an informed judgment.

I am indebted to many people in the preparation of this work, especially to the scholars who have done the hard research behind this book. I give them few specific credits in the text itself. To keep things simple I use no footnotes or references. The list of sources at the end of this book provides the names and works of these scholars, and the annotations suggest their main arguments and the history of the scholarly discussion. Anyone interested in further detail will find ample resources there.

I rely most heavily on the work of John Boswell, Professor of History at Yale University, and L. William Countryman, Professor of New Testament at the Church Divinity School of the Pacific, Berkeley, California. They have argued most cogently for a reinterpretation of the Bible texts on "homosexuality." Boswell's meticulous study of biblical terms pushed the scholarship to a new level of clarity, and Countryman's analysis of purity issues in Romans transformed the discussion. Countryman's is the most recent lengthy study and has taken all the others into account. For the most part, this book merely reports the original historical research of Boswell and Countryman.

However, I depart from Boswell and Countryman in my treatment of 1 Corinthians 6:9 and 1 Timothy 1:10, and I rely more heavily on Robin Scroggs, Professor of New Testament at Union Theological Seminary, New York City; David F. Wright, Senior Lecturer in Ecclesiatical History and former Dean of the Faculty of Divinity at New College, The University of Edinburgh, Scotland; William L. Petersen, Associate Professor of Religious Studies at The Pennsylvania State University; and Victor P. Furnish, University Distinguished Professor of New Testament at Perkins School of Theology, Southern Methodist University. Debate revolves around an obscure Greek term, *arsenokoitai*, and the weight of historical evidence suggests this term does intend some kind of male same-sex acts.

I am also grateful to other colleagues and friends—especially to Bishop John S. Spong for his gracious and kind Foreword to this book, to Mike Bathum for collaboration on an early idea to provide illustrations for this book, to Steven Tomlinson for very helpful suggestions on a number of successive drafts, and to Ricardo Langoria, Scott Moore, and Paul Whitaker Paré for extensive and detailed criticism on an early draft. I thank Bert Herrman of Alamo Square Press for his willingness to publish this Bible study and for his meticulous attention to this book at every stage of the publishing process. For feedback, criticism, ideas, information, encouragement and motivation, I thank Mark Adcox, Cheryl Amendola, John Dennis Anderson, Kerry Baker, Richard Beauchesne, Sylvia Chavez, L. William Countryman, H. Thomas Cunningham, Paul Dauben, James R. DeMuth (R.I.P.), Michael H. Floyd, James Michael Flynn, Jesse Gomez, C. Edward Harris, Jan Heemrood, David Henton, Bruce Jarstfer, Toby Johnson, David Jones, Frank Leclerc (R.I.P.), Raymond Machesney, Richard N. Marshall, Donna Mayfield, Don McMahon, Christopher Menzel, Robert Nugent, William L. Petersen, Paula Rieder, William C. Spong, John Tessaro, Elisa Velasquez and John Welch. Of course, I take full responsibility for what is finally written here.

22

One. Introduction

A millennium ago, Western society was rather indifferent to homosexuality and even supportive of it. A gay subculture thrived. Clerics and nuns wrote love letters and poetry to one another. All of Europe delighted in the romance of Richard the Lion-Hearted of England and Philip, the king of France. Students at the newly founded Christian universities regularly debated the pros and cons of straight versus gay love. And no law codes in Europe (except in Visigoth Spain) included prohibitions of homosexual acts.

By the middle of the eleven hundreds, things began to change. Peter Cantor campaigned for condemnation of gay love affairs among the clergy. Contrary to all precedence, he restricted the term sodomy to refer to same-sex acts and interpreted Romans 1:26-27 to refer exclusively to homosexuality. In contrast to the experience of Richard and Philip and just a little more than a century later, Edward II of England was assassinated for his gay relationship with Hugh le Despenser. In 1179, Lateran III became the first ecumenical church council to require punishment for homosexual acts. This change was part of a growing intolerance that was coming over Europe. Order and uniformity became the rule of the day, and volumes and volumes of law codes were promulgated. For the first time in Christian history, Jews and Muslims were persecuted, the poor were regarded as a menace, and, in a crusade in southern France and through the Inquisition, "heretics" were put to death. At the same time, homosexuals began to face violent and open opposition. Thus began a millennium of Christian condemnation of homosexuality.

John Boswell, the late Yale historian, researched that history. He also commented that the 20th Century has been the most virulently anti-gay of all. In pre-World War II Germany, the Nazis destroyed Magnus Hirschfeld's Institute for Sex Research, along with its thousands of case studies and massive research library, and began sending homosexuals to concentration camps.

In its first 25 years, the Metropolitan Community Church, a nation-wide, and now international, denomination founded to minister especially to gay and lesbian people, suffered 18 church burnings, including one in New Orleans in 1973, in which 29 people died and which national news media virtually ignored.

From January 1999 to June 1999, 43 men and women were murdered in anti-gay hate crimes in the United States. These are in addition to the well known pistol whipping and crucifixion of 21-year-old Matthew Shepard and the beating and burning of 39-year-old Billy Jack Gaither. Since Anita Bryant's successful 1977 campaign to repeal a gay rights ordinance in Dade County, Florida, the religious right has become increasingly vocal in opposition to homosexuality.

At the same time, however, other recent occurrences have gradually been more supportive of lesbian and gay people. Laws are on the books in many places to guarantee civil rights in jobs, housing and child care, and companies and municipalities continue to add a sexual-orientation clause to their nondiscrimination policies. Programs for domestic benefits, which can apply to same-sex couples, are available in universities, businesses and government agencies. Gay and lesbian figures are common in the news, movies, TV programs and entertainment, and social reports. Public opinion is gradually shifting toward greater understanding and acceptance of homosexual, bisexual and transgender people.

Slowly the intolerance of the last millennium is being reversed. But debate continues to rage in religious circles. In many cases it is splitting denominations down the middle. And of course, at center stage stands the Bible with its many interpreters.

People quote the Bible to back up their opposition to homosexuality. But others claim the matter is not as simple as that. They also believe in the Bible, but they do not believe the Bible condemns lesbian and gay sex.

This book is to help you form your own opinion on the matter. For the past 25 to 30 years, professional scripture scholars have been studying homosexuality in the Bible. Research is now at a point where we can make a brief and accurate summary that lay people can understand. Such a summary is what you are now reading.

The social sciences indicate that anywhere from two to four percent of the population is *exclusively* homosexual; that is, they experience romantic attraction only toward members of their own sex. Some further proportion of the population is *predominantly* homosexual; that is, for the most part they are attracted to people of the same sex. Added together, these two groups make up the well publicized "ten percent" said to be homosexual. But the first group alone, the two to four percent, is a significant number of people. In comparison, recall that the Jewish population in the United States is between two to three percent of the total.

Many of those who are homosexual have been raised to believe in the Bible, and they have been told that it condemns homosexuality. They are really in a bind. Their family and friends, who know they are good people, also feel caught in a bind. It looks as if homosexual people have to give up their religion or else—which seems impossible—give up their sexuality.

That is no small matter. In fact, scientific study of sexuality, along with psychology, has been underway for barely a century. But it is already clear that sexuality goes to the core of a person.

Sexuality means much more than physical arousal and orgasm. Attached to a person's sexuality is the capacity to feel affection, to delight in someone else, to get emotionally close to another person, to be passionately committed to him or her. Sexuality is at the core of that marvelous human experience, being in love—to be struck by the beauty of another and be drawn out of yourself, to become attached to another human being so powerfully that you easily begin measuring your life in terms of what's good for someone else as well as for yourself.

Sexuality is part and parcel of the human capacity for love. For we are not just intellectual beings, making calculated decisions to cherish somebody; we are emotional and physical, too. All this is what it means to be a human being, and all this comes into play when human love is on the scene.

To have to be afraid to feel sexual is to restrain that noblest of human possibilities, love. It is to short-circuit human spontaneity in a whole array of expressions—creativity, motivation, passion, commitment, heroic achievement. It is to be afraid of part of one's own deepest self.

This is not to say that sex acts are a necessary part of every human love. This is not to say that people cannot live without having sex. It is only to say that people who are afraid of their sexuality are constantly in hiding from their own selves. As a result, they are handicapped in all their dealings with other people and especially in their capacity to love deeply. All interior growth is stunted when people repress their affection, for heartfelt passion is really the engine of human achievement.

So, in a profound and important way, for people to have to choose between religion and sexuality is to have to choose between religion and themselves. As we are coming to understand the matter today, it is to have to choose between God and human wholeness.

That choice seems too hard, and it does not seem to make sense. Mounting scientific evidence shows it is nobody's doing that people are lesbian or gay. There is no reason to believe that homosexuality in itself is in any way unhealthy. And there is no credible evidence that sexual orientation can be changed nor convincing argument that it should be. The sociological, the psychological, the biological evidence, all more and more surely points in the same direction. The fact is that some people just happen to be homosexual.

Most people are straight but some are lesbian, gay or bisexual. Some people are tall, and some are small. Some are black or brown, others are yellow, red or white. Some are men, more are women. Most are right-handed, but some are left-handed. There is a wide range of individual differences among human beings. Sexual orientation seems to be one of those differences.

According to faith, it is God who creates us. Divine Providence forms us as we are. Our genes, our temperaments, our time and place in history, our talents, our gifts, our strengths and weaknesses—all are part of God's inscrutable and loving plan for us. So somehow God must be behind the fact that some people are homosexual. Then why should God's word in the Bible condemn homosexuality? There must be a mistake in the reasoning somewhere.

Could it be that *they* are the mistake? That something has gone wrong with lesbian and gay people? That they are inherently flawed? Some would believe so. But then God must be evil or be playing some cruel trick, but that cannot be. God does not make junk. So there must be another answer.

The mistake must be in how the Bible is being read. This is the argument presented here.

This book looks into the matter. The investigation begins with a discussion of methods of interpreting the Bible. That discussion is perhaps the most important part of this book, for how one reads the Bible is the heart of the matter. In perfectly good faith, two different people reading the same text can come up with two different meanings. Understand how different approaches to the Bible can lead to very different conclusions and you have an illuminating perspective on the debates about homosexuality in the Bible or about any other biblical topic.

Chapter Two explains those different ways of reading the Bible. Chapters Three through Seven consider each of the Bible texts that supposedly talk about homosexuality. Chapter Eight deals with other biblical arguments about homosexuality, such as the implications of the Bible's positive teaching about heterosexuality and Jesus' reaction to a same-sex relationship. Finally, Chapter Nine summarizes the conclusion of this investigation.

This popular presentation of the Bible's real teaching about homosexuality should help reverse the hostility of the second millennium and restore a Christ-like openness to all God's children. Then the charity that characterized earlier Christianity might again color Christianity in the third millennium.

Two. Interpreting the Bible

People differ passionately about what the Bible actually teaches. What's going on? Who is right?

Who is right? It depends on how one reads the Bible!

What's going on? Different ways of reading the Bible!

How one reads the Bible, the way one interprets the texts—this is the key issue. The question is not, "What are the Bible texts on homosexuality?" Anyone could list and quote them. The question is, "How do you interpret these texts?" "How do you determine what these texts really mean?"

Some will say we should take the Bible as it reads and not "interpret" it. But "interpretation" simply means getting the meaning out of a text. In this sense, there is no reading the Bible or anything else without interpreting. Without a reader, a text is only words—markings on a page. In themselves these markings mean nothing. To have meaning, they have to pass through someone's mind. Understanding the words, determining the meaning of the text, is interpretation. Any time people read anything, they are interpreting.

Words Don't Always Mean What They Say

It is important to pay attention to the different ways of reading a text, especially when dealing with ancient texts, like the Bible. The words might suggest one thing to us in the 21st Century but have meant something very different to the people who wrote them long ago.

Take an example from everyday life. In the United States we have an expression: to be out in left field. To understand this expression you have to know something about baseball. Areas of the baseball field are called center, right and left field, as viewed from the batter's position. Most batters are right-handed. They swing from right to left. So they tend to hit the ball more often and more deeply into left field. When they do hit a ball into right field, the ball is not likely to go as far. So the player covering left field needs to be positioned far back in the field, far from the other players. In many ways the left fielder is isolated and out of touch, off in his or her own world. So to say someone is "out in left field" means he or she is disoriented, out of contact with reality, wrong, unconventional, loony.

Now, what if you spoke perfectly good English but knew nothing of baseball or American usage and you heard that expression for the first time? "You're wondering about Robert? He's out in left field." You might go out looking for Robert in a field somewhere off to the left! You understood the words, but you missed the point.

Of course, you could argue that the words mean what they say. You heard them, and you did understand them. They locate Robert in a field that is "left," and "left" is a direction opposite "right." After all, you do speak English! You could insist if you wanted, but everybody else would think *you're* out in left field.

Baseball was really the big thing in the '40s and '50s. Other concerns have since shared the scene. So to make the same point in the '60s and '70s, you might have said, "You're a real space cadet." Today you might say, "You just don't compute" or "You're 404" (from the Worldwide web error message, "404 Not found" : the requested document could not be located).

Those sayings have nothing to do with real fields, space travel or computers, and they all make the same point. But ignore the culture in which they belong and you'll miss the point despite understanding the words.

Jesus' Teaching about Simplicity

Take an example from the Bible. In three of the Gospels—Matthew 19:24, Mark 10:25 and Luke 18:25—Jesus says, "It is easier for a camel to pass through the eye of a needle than for a rich person to enter the kingdom of God." It sounds as if nobody who had lots of money could ever get into heaven, for certainly no camel could ever get through a needle's eye. At least that's what this saying suggests to us.

But some scholars have pointed out that in Jerusalem there was a very low and narrow gate through the city wall. When a caravan entered through that gate, the camels had to be unloaded, led through the gate crouching down, and then reloaded inside the city wall. That gate was supposedly called "the eye of the needle."

So what was Jesus saying? Understand something about his everyday world, and his meaning is obvious. Jesus was simply saying that it would be hard for the rich to get to heaven. They might first have to unload their material concerns. Jesus was again preaching his Sermon-on-the-Mount message about simplicity of life and single-heartedness.

What if similar considerations apply to the Bible texts on homosexuality? Maybe those texts do not mean what we have been taking them to mean.

Alternative Interpretations

Of course, the Gospels recount that the disciples objected to Jesus' teaching about the eye of the needle. "Then who could be saved?" they protested. And Jesus responded that nothing is impossible with God.

So you could take Jesus' teaching to apply to a real physical impossibility, to a real camel passing through the eye of a real needle. You could insist that God could work a miracle, if God wanted to. You could insist that this text is actually about trusting God to do what seems impossible. And your interpretation would, indeed, fit the text.

But now we have two very different interpretations. And we have two very different pictures—not only of the text in question but also different pictures of God, of Jesus and of religious faith.

One interpretation appeals to miracles. It portrays a God who intervenes to suspend the laws of the universe, and it sees Jesus as teaching faith in such a God. This interpretation presents a picture of people entering heaven because God stepped in to work a miracle in their lives. The other interpretation appeals to Divine Providence. It portrays a God who works through the ordinary functioning of the universe, and it sees Jesus calling us to live responsibly in this world. This other interpretation presents a picture of people entering heaven because they unloaded the false concerns that burden their lives.

Both pictures do allow that God is guiding our lives and our world. But when it comes to the crunch, the one expects a miracle from God, and it awaits a vision or a revelation to settle a question. The other approach, more down-to-earth, presumes that God is already and always working through things as they are and it is up to us to make the best of the circumstances God has allowed. The down-to-earth approach is not irreligious. It is brimming with trust in God. It embraces the world as God made it. It uses the intelligence God gave us. It resolves questions by honest appeal to the evidence. It makes decisions in loving concern for what is right and good. In sum, it accepts our God-given stewardship over the world and over our lives.

Is one approach better than the other? Well, the core Judeo-Christian beliefs support the down-to-earth approach. God created our world and saw that it was good. God's Son came down to earth and lived among us. Jesus did not expect God to save him from death, and God did not. Evidently, according to biblical teaching and apart from human misuse, the world that God created and redeemed is good enough for God. Should it not also be good enough for us? Should we not also be down-to-earth in our faith?

Of course, the Bible does portray God as working miracles. And to pray for a miracle is not wrong—unless there is no need for one. But when there is no need, Jesus' words to Satan apply to us: "Do not put the Lord your God to the test" (Matthew 4:7; Luke 4:12). Besides, if we actually believed that God is working in our lives regardless of how things go, would we ever really feel the need to pray for a miracle?

Might we not be testing God by reading a miraculous interpretation into the text about the eye of the needle? A perfectly reasonable alternative interpretation is available. To insist, nonetheless, on a miraculous interpretation—isn't this acting on whim? Isn't this expecting God to do extraordinary things simply because we would prefer it so?

The Literal Reading and the Historical-Critical Reading

This book will focus on two different approaches to interpreting the Bible: the "literal reading" and the "historical-critical" reading. These two are parallels to the miraculous and the down-to-earth approaches to religion.

The literal reading claims to take the text simply for what it says. This is the approach of Biblical Fundamentalism. It claims not to be interpreting the text but merely to be reading it as it stands. Clearly, however, even Fundamentalism follows a rule of interpretation, a simple and easy rule. The rule is that a text means whatever it means to somebody reading it today.

Compare the other approach, the historical-critical reading. The rule here is that a text means whatever it meant to the people who wrote it long ago. To say what a biblical text teaches us today, you first have to understand the text in its original situation and then apply the meaning to the present situation. Jesus' teaching about the eye of the needle, in the down-to-earth approach, is a good example.

Although on TV and radio we generally hear only the Fundamentalist approach, all the mainline Christian churches support the historical-critical method. So the argument being presented here is not novel; on the contrary, it is absolutely standard and has almost two centuries of study behind it. In fact, it was on the scene before Fundamentalism, which arose partially in opposition to it.

Of course, some of the churches back off from the historical-critical method when it comes to the Bible texts on homosexuality and some other questions—like divorce, the place of women in society and church, Jesus' understanding of himself, the organization of the early church, or the origin of Christian rituals like Baptism and Eucharist. The churches are wary of the conclusions that their own approved method of interpretation suggests.

Historical-critical study of the Bible oftentimes reverses some long-standing interpretations and raises very serious questions about religion and society. No wonder the churches are hesitant. They are sometimes left wondering what to teach. No wonder Biblical Fundamentalism has taken a harder line. The new historical input can leave the older understanding of religion dissolving before our eyes. It is important to appreciate the delicateness of this matter of biblical interpretation.

But it is also important not to hide from the facts as we now know them. To do so would be to violate a core value of the Judeo-Christian tradition. To do so would be to ignore a value for which Jesus lived and died—even as John 8:32 has Jesus say, "The truth will set you free."

This approach is called "historical" because it requires that you put the text back into its original historical and cultural context before you decide what it means. This approach is called "critical" because it requires careful thought and detailed analysis of the Bible. The word critical is not used here in the more familiar sense of "trying to find fault with something" but in the sense of the current phrase, *critical thinking.*

Inspiration and Inerrancy of the Bible

These two ways of reading the Bible are very different, but both agree that the Bible is God's word. Both agree that God inspired the Bible and that the Bible is "inerrant" or without error. So no one can dismiss the historical-critical approach by claiming that it does not respect the Bible as God's word. Of course, those two approaches explain inspiration and inerrancy differently.

Inspiration means that God moved the human authors to write what they wrote, so the Bible is God's word to us. The literal approach relies on miracles, so for it inspiration means that God's power overwhelmed the human authors. The words just flowed from them. Sometimes the human authors did not even understand what they were writing. Now we, centuries later, can recognize in the Bible a secret message that God miraculously hid there for our generation alone.

The historical-critical approach understands biblical inspiration differently. This approach will agree that what the human authors wrote may well have further meaning of which they themselves were not aware. But for the historical-critical approach, the mentality is down-to-earth. People often say things that mean more than they know, especially when they speak eternal truths of the heart—like "A thing of beauty is a joy forever" or "I will love you as long as I live" or "Trust in God, and all will be well." So as history unfolds, the Bible texts will naturally suggest new and deeper meanings. The most obvious example is how the early Christians saw references to Jesus in the Hebrew Scriptures.

Moreover, according to the historical-critical approach, the biblical writers were not entranced secretaries, taking dictation like robots or channelling messages as in a seance. Rather, the biblical authors were well aware of what they were writing. They were intelligent, free, creative, culture-bound human beings. And God respected all that. God used all that, their humanity and their culture, to express divine wisdom in a particular human form. Thus, what they wrote is not only their word but also the word of God. Accordingly, if you wanted to understand what God intended to say, the first step would be to understand what those human authors intended to say. For precisely that is what God inspired.

Granted that the Bible is the word of God, the Bible must be free from error. Thus, the question of biblical inerrancy enters the discussion. Again, the literal and the historical-critical approaches both accept inerrancy, but they understand it differently.

The literal approach would take words to mean exactly what they say. Hearing that Robert is a real space cadet, this approach would assume that he is truly a NASA astronaut. Similarly, reading in the first chapter of Genesis that God created the world in seven days, the literal approach would insist that the universe was formed in one week. For if creation did not happen that way, the Bible is mistaken.

In contrast, the historical-critical approach first asks, What is the point of the Genesis story of creation? What was the author intending to say? Well, the Bible intended to give a religion lesson, not a science lesson. The seven-day story of creation is just a way of making the point: God created the universe with wisdom, care and order. If science determines that the universe actually evolved over millions and millions of years, there is no conflict with the Bible. Through science we are simply coming to understand how God chose to create the world. Science helps us to grasp some bit of the order and wisdom that God built into the universe. But the fact that God created the universe remains as true as ever. There is no error in that teaching of Genesis.

Both the literal approach and the historical-critical approach hold that the Bible is God's word, inspired and inerrant. There is no disagreement here. But these two approaches do disagree on what is exactly God's word in the Bible. For God's "word" is not the markings on the page nor even the string of words in the sentences. Rather, God's word is the *meaning* of the words and sentences formed by the markings on the page. Disagreeing on how to determine what the Bible means, the two approaches disagree on what God's inspired and inerrant word is. They disagree about what the Bible teaches because they interpret the Bible differently.

Pluses and Minuses of the Literal Approach

These two approaches to interpreting the Bible have their advantages and disadvantages. Consider first the literal approach. It is easy. It has no elaborate guidelines. It appeals to common sense and requires no detailed study. All this is clearly an advantage—at least in the short run—because it makes religion simple.

But the literal reading also has disadvantages. Since this approach has no elaborate guidelines, different people can arrive at different meanings for any text they consider. All can claim that the text means what it means to them.

Then how do you settle the differences of opinion? In the end, the text will be taken to mean what any group of people come to agree on. Popularity decides what the Bible means. An influential preacher could even impose a personal view on a whole congregation.

But the fact that many people believe something, doesn't necessarily make it right. The long history of slavery is a clear case in point. So the serious disadvantage here is that people may well end up believing not what God requires but simply what makes them comfortable and secure.

Another disadvantage is selective use of the Bible. That is, this approach tends to emphasize one text and overlook another. Preachers condemn lesbians and gays because the Bible mentions same-sex acts in passing. But the same preachers do not advocate slavery even though many long passages support it (Ephesians 6:5-9; Colossians 3:22-4:1; 1 Timothy 6:1-2; 1 Peter 2:18). They do not encourage people to gouge out their eyes or cut off their hands even though Jesus' literal words suggest that remedy for temptation (Matthew 5:22-29). Those preachers often allow divorce even though Jesus' teaching taken literally condemns it (Matthew 5:32; Mark 10:1-12; Luke 16:18). They allow women to teach in Sunday school or to speak in church even though 1 Timothy 2:11-14 clearly forbids that. They allow women to come to church in expensive clothes or gold jewelry or pearls or to come to church without hats even though long passages oppose such things (1 Timothy 2:9-10; 1 Corinthians 11:1-16). They use banks and profit from loans and investments even though the Bible forbids the taking of interest (Exodus 22:25; Psalm 15:15, Proverbs 28:8; Ezekial 18:13, 17, 22:12). They do not believe the earth is flat as Genesis 1:1-17 suggests.The literal approach is almost forced to pick and choose as it applies the Bible. Otherwise some very unacceptable situations would arise.

Finally, the literal approach is hard pressed to address new issues— nuclear energy, surrogate motherhood, environmental pollution, the use of outer space, genetic engineering, regulation of the Internet. The Bible never imagined these things, so it never really addressed them.

Of course, some will insist that God did speak of these things in hidden and symbolic ways. Some will claim that certain obscure Bible texts were really speaking about issues of our day. But if this is so, in some cases a symbolic interpretation is allowed, and the rule of literal interpretation is abandoned. Then what is the rule for knowing when to interpret literally and when to interpret symbolically? Without changing rules in the middle of the game, the literal approach cannot use the Bible to answer pressing questions of our day.

Pluses and Minuses of the Historical-Critical Approach

The historical-critical method also has its advantages and its disadvantages. On the positive side, this approach can determine the meaning of a text objectively, following clear guidelines. All who accept this method can agree on the interpretation.

Because of this approach, there are now no important differences between Catholic and Protestant Bible scholars. All are in general agreement about the meaning of Bible texts. When differences do occur, they do not depend on one's Protestant or Catholic affiliation. The differences depend on the historical evidence scholars cite and on the arguments they propose.

The line that divides the Christian churches no longer falls between Catholics and Protestants. The line of division falls between those who follow a literal reading of the Bible and those who follow an historical-critical reading, and this line often cuts right through the middle of a single church or denomination.

That God really is working in human history, not somehow floating above it, is a core aspect of Judeo-Christian faith. So another advantage of the historical-critical method is that it takes history and God's working in history seriously. As history progresses, God guides the process and things really do change. There is development and novelty. According to this understanding, religion is not locked into its first-century form.

However, the historical-critical method has a serious disadvantage. It is not easy. It requires long and difficult study. Only specialists can apply it. This method makes Bible interpretation a technical science. Archeology, history, ancient languages, anthropology, minute analysis of words and texts are all required for proper interpretation.

And some texts will be left forever unexplained. If all memory of baseball were suddenly lost, no one might ever understand what being "out in left field" means. Likewise, if the historical information around some Bible text is lacking, we may never be able to determine what the text meant to say. The discussion about two texts in Chapter Seven, 1 Corinthians 6:9 and 1 Timothy 1:10, offers a good example. The historical evidence on these texts remains very, very scanty. Historical argument can become very tenuous—simply because we may not have the historical information to determine what a crucial word or phrase was supposed to mean.

Moreover, according to the historical-critical method, the times really do change. We cannot expect to find simple answers to contemporary questions just by reading the Bible. To understand God's will for us, we have to apply the lessons of the past to the problems of today. So, besides knowing what the Bible meant, we have to study the current problem. Sensitive to God's Spirit, we have to rely on our own minds and hearts to decide what the Bible requires in the situations we now face. To do that, we have to be good people—open, honest and loving or, in a word: authentic. All this is very demanding.

Finally, it is possible that this method of reading the Bible may overturn long-accepted interpretations. It may turn out that some Bible texts do not mean what we took them to mean for centuries. Then difficult debate about sensitive social issues arises. Homosexuality is an obvious case in point.

What about Homosexuality in the Bible?

This book summarizes recent Bible research on homosexuality following the historical-critical method. Based on our understanding of historical-critical method, what conclusion about homosexuality should we expect? Consider the facts.

The scientific study of sexuality is barely a century old. We now know that homosexuality is a core aspect of the personality, probably fixed by early childhood, biologically based, and affecting a significant proportion of the population in virtually every known culture. There is no convincing evidence that sexual orientation can be changed, and there is no evidence whatsoever that homosexuality is in any way pathological. Since the Second World War a worldwide gay community has been forming and gaining a voice. Within that community, and especially among gay and lesbian religious people, loving, adult homosexual relationships have become a major concern.

All those developments are recent. Some of them are absolutely new to human history. They are part of a situation that the biblical authors never imagined, so it is not to be expected that the Bible expresses an opinion about them. What is to be expected is this: When the Bible does talk about same-sex behavior, it refers to it as it was understood in those ancient times. The biblical teachings will apply today only insofar as the ancient understanding of same-sex behavior is still valid.

Specifically, in biblical times there was no elaborated understanding of *homosexuality* as a sexual orientation. The ancient Israelites did not even think about sex in these terms. There was only a general awareness of same-sex contacts or same-sex acts, what can be called *homogenitality* and *homogenital* acts. Our question today is about people and their relationships, not simply about sex acts. Our question is about *homosexuality*, a particular way of being human, not mere *homogenitality*, the engagement in same-sex acts. Our question is about spontaneous affection for people of the same sex and about the ethical possibility of expressing that affection in sexual relationships. Because this was not a question in the minds of the biblical authors, we cannot expect the Bible to give an answer.

Why must that be so? If the Bible condemned a particular act for whatever reason, shouldn't that act still be avoided without any further discussion? If God's word says it is wrong, isn't it wrong, period?

A thing is wrong for a reason. If the reason no longer holds and no other reason is given, how can a thing still be judged wrong? Simply that "God said it is wrong" is not a good enough answer, for the point remains even in the case of God: God also says things are wrong for reasons. That is to say, there is good sense, there is wisdom, in the morality that God requires. If there is not, then all morality is arbitrary, and God makes things right or wrong on divine whim. Then all thought about ethics should stop, for there would simply be no rationale to morality; there would be no reasonableness in what God requires. But such a conclusion is absurd. It is absolutely ridiculous. So there must be a reason why something is wrong, and it must be for that very reason that God forbids the thing.

Well, couldn't God have reasons that we cannot understand? Of course. But if that is the case, we could never know God's will—unless God revealed it to us. And where would God reveal it? One obvious answer is, "In the Bible, of course!"

That answer is perfectly valid. But it brings us right back to our starting point: How do we determine what God meant to say in the Bible? The options are still the same: the literal approach or the historical-critical approach.

This book deliberately follows the historical-critical approach to the Bible. The expectation is that God says something is wrong for a reason. The Creator built that reason into the structure of the universe. Human intelligence would be able to discern that reason. Accordingly, when there is no new reason for a thing's being wrong and a former reason no longer applies, there is no basis for saying the thing is wrong. The reason— *God's own reason!* —is simply not there.

Does God's word in the Bible condemn what we know today as homosexuality? Consider all the biblical passages that refer to this topic. Understand them in their original historical context. Evaluate the evidence with an open and honest mind. The text-by-text analysis that follows will help you draw your own conclusion.

Three. The Sin of Sodom: Inhospitality

The story of Sodom is probably the most famous Bible passage that deals with homosexuality—or, at least, is said to deal with it. This story is found in the book of Genesis, chapter 19, verses 1 to 11:

> The two angels came to Sodom in the evening; and Lot was sitting in the gateway of Sodom. When Lot saw them, he rose to meet them, and bowed down with his face to the ground. He said, "Please, my lords, turn aside to your servant's house and spend the night, and wash your feet; then you can rise early and go on your way." They said, "No; we will spend the night in the square." But he urged them strongly; so they turned aside to him and entered his house; and he made them a feast, and baked unleavened bread, and they ate. But before they lay down, the men of the city, the men of Sodom, both young and old, all the people to the last man, surrounded the house; and they called to Lot, "Where are the men who came to you tonight? Bring them out to us, so that we may know them." Lot went out of the door to the men, shut the door after him, and said, "I beg you, my brothers, do not act so wickedly. Look, I have two daughters who have not known a man; let me bring them out to you, and

do to them as you please; only do nothing to these men, for they have come under the shelter of my roof." But they replied, "Stand back!" And they said, "This fellow came here as an alien [Lot was not originally from Sodom], and he would play the judge! Now we will deal worse with you than with them." Then they pressed hard against the man Lot, and came near the door to break it down. But the men inside reached out their hands and brought Lot into the house with them, and shut the door. And they struck with blindness the men who were at the door of the house, both small and great, so that they were unable to find the door.

The visiting angels then warned Lot that God was going to destroy Sodom in a downpour of fire and brimstone. So Lot and his family escaped the town. However, Lot's wife disobeyed the command not to look back, and she was turned into a pillar of salt. Sodom and neighboring Gomorrah were destroyed, "and lo, the smoke of the land went up like the smoke of a furnace" (19:28).

A Common Interpretation of the Story

Since about the 12th Century, this story has been commonly taken to condemn homosexuality. The very word "sodomite" was taken to refer to someone who engages in anal sex, and the sin of Sodom was taken to be male homogenital acts. So supposedly God condemned and punished the citizens of Sodom, the Sodomites, for homogenital activity.

What Does "To Know" Mean?

Indeed, there is a clear sexual reference in the story. Lot offers his daughters as sex objects to the men crowding around his door. His daughters were virgins. Lot said they did not know a man.

In the Bible, "to know" sometimes means "to have sex with." That is the meaning of the word in the Christian Testament (also known as the "New Testament") where the angel told Mary that she was to be the mother of Jesus. Mary wondered, "How can this happen, since I do not *know* man" (Luke 1:34)? The verb "to know" occurs some 943 times in the Hebrew Testament (also known as the "Old Testament"). In ten of those cases the word has a sexual meaning. The present text is one of those ten.

It is shocking to think that Lot would have offered his daughters to the Sodomites. This is a good example of how different Lot's culture was from our own. In that time the father of the house actually owned the women. They were his property. He was free do with them almost whatever he wanted. It would have been very costly for Lot to give his daughters to those men, financially costly. For no one would then want to marry those women, already "used." It is surprising that Lot preferred to let the men of the town rape his daughters than to let them abuse his houseguests.

What did the men of Sodom want with Lot's two visitors? They say they wanted "to know them." Some take this to mean the men wanted to have sex with the visitors. Lot's offering his daughters for sex in place of the male visitors certainly indicates as much. Still, others argue the word "to know" need not refer to sex. It may simply be that the men of Sodom wanted to find out who these strangers were and what they were doing in their town. After all, Lot was not a native of Sodom. He, too, was an outsider. The townsfolk were not happy with his inviting strangers in.

In the end there is no way of being absolutely certain whether this text refers to homogenital acts or not. In fact, most experts believe that it does. What is certain is that this text is concerned about abuse, not simply about sex.

As we will see below, in the many biblical references to the sin of Sodom, there is no concern whatsoever about homogenitality, but there is concern about hardheartedness and abuse. Allowing that the word "to know" really does have a sexual meaning here, what is at stake is male-male rape, not simply male-male sex.

The Duty of Hospitality

Why would Lot have been willing to expose his daughters to rape? Why would Lot object to the townsfolk interrogating and abusing the visitors? Lot was a just man or, as the Scriptures say, a righteous man. He did what was right, as best he could. Of all the people in Sodom, only he had the kindness to invite the travelers in for the night.

In desert country, where Sodom lay, to stay outside exposed to the cold of the night could be fatal. So a cardinal rule of Lot's society was to offer hospitality to travelers. The same rule is a traditional part of Semitic and Arabic cultures. This rule was so strict that no one might harm even an enemy who had been offered shelter for the night. So doing what was right, following God's law as he understood it, Lot refused to expose his guests to the abuse of the men of Sodom. To do so would have violated the law of sacred hospitality.

The Meaning of Male Anal Sex

If, in addition, the Sodomites did want sex with the town visitors, the offense against them would have been multiplied. For forcing sex on men was a way of humiliating them. During war, for example, besides raping the women and slaughtering the children, the victors would often also "sodomize" the defeated soldiers. The idea was to insult the men by treating them like women. So part and parcel of the practice of male-male anal sex was the notion that men should be "macho" and that women are inferior, pieces of property at the service of men.

In fact, throughout Western history, a main reason for opposition to male-male sex was that it supposedly makes a man act like a woman. Saint John Chrysostom in the East and Saint Augustine in the West in the Fifth Century and Peter Cantor in the 12th, outspoken Christian opponents of homogenitality, both raised that argument. Saint Augustine wrote, "The body of a man is as superior to that of a woman as the soul is to the body." To be the active partner was generally more acceptable, but to be the receptive partner was "unmanly." Evidently, the objection was more to a man's being "effeminate" than to his having sex with another man.

The Sin of Sodom

So what was the sin of Sodom? Abuse and offense against strangers. Insult to the traveler. Inhospitality to the needy. That is the point of the story understood in its own historical context.

When male-male rape becomes part of the story, the additional offense is sexual abuse—gross insult and humiliation in Lot's time and in

46

our own. The whole story and its culture make clear that the author was not concerned about sex in itself, and it was irrelevant whether the sex was hetero- or homosexual. In place of his male guests, without a second thought Lot offered his daughters. The point of the story is not sexual ethics. The story of Sodom is no more about sex than it is about pounding on someone's front door. In the story of Sodom, both the sex and the pounding are incidental to the main point of the story. The point is abuse and assault, in whatever form they take. To use this text to condemn homosexuality is to misuse this text.

Judges 19 tells another story that is an obvious parallel to the story of Sodom. A Levite who was traveling with his servant and concubine needed shelter for the night. He sat in the town square at Gibeah. No one offered him hospitality except a foreigner who was living in that town. When they were all inside, the men of the town assaulted the house and demanded to have sex with the Levite. Just as Lot did, the host protested, "No, my brothers, do not act so wickedly. Since this man is my guest, do not do this vile thing." The host offered his virgin daughter to the townsmen, but they did not want her. Then the Levite pushed out his concubine, and the townsmen raped her all through the night. In the morning, she lay dead on the doorstep of the house. In punishment, all the tribes of Israel collected an army and destroyed the town of Gibeah.

Clearly, the story of the Levite's concubine is indifferent to homosexuality or heterosexuality—as is the story of Sodom. A man or a woman would serve as equally valid sex objects. And rape in either case was equally heinous. Sexual orientation is not the point. In fact, neither is the sex. In both stories, the sexual assault only serves to highlight the wickedness of the townspeople. The people of Gibeah and of Sodom are condemned for their meanness, cruelty, and abuse. Not homosexuality but hardheartedness is the offense of Gibeah and of Sodom.

The Bible's Own Understanding of the Sin of Sodom

That is the conclusion that follows from an historical-critical reading of the Sodom story. But in this particular case the meaning of the text is obvious from other parts of the Bible. For the Bible often refers back to the story of Sodom and says outright what Sodom's sin was.

The prophet Ezekiel (16:48-49) states the case baldly. "This was the guilt of your sister Sodom: she and her daughters had pride, surfeit of food and prosperous ease, but did not aid the poor and needy." The sin of the Sodomites was that they refused to take in the needy travelers.

Some people would like to see homosexuality in that text. They point out that the word *abomination* occurs throughout this chapter of Ezekiel and even in verse 50, right after the verse about Sodom. They understand this to refer to the abomination of Leviticus 18:22: "You shall not lie with a male as with a woman; it is an abomination" (see Chapter Four).

But in the Hebrew Scriptures the word *abomination* is used to refer to many things. The abomination in question here is Jerusalem's "adultery" and "harlotry," and these words are being used symbolically. They do not refer to sexual acts but to idolatry, to Israel's infidelity to God, and to child sacrifice and murder. Even though verse 50 mentions "abominable things" and is referring to Sodom, verse 49 says exactly what the abominable things in this case were. It says outright what the wickedness of Sodom was, and male-male sex is simply not mentioned. Chapter 16 of Ezekial is clearly about other things.

According to Wisdom 19:13, the sin of Sodom was a "bitter hatred of strangers" and "making slaves of guests who were benefactors." Recall that the strangers, the guests, were actually angels on mission from God. The sin was to treat them abusively. The reference to "making slaves of guests" may refer to a common practice of the day wherein the master of a house would freely use the slaves for sexual purposes. But again, the offense was not in having sex nor even in keeping slaves but in taking advantage of, demeaning and abusing others.

Even Jesus makes reference to Sodom, and the issue is rejection of God's messengers:

> These twelve Jesus sent out with the following instructions: ". . . Whatever town or village you enter, find out who in it is worthy, and stay there until you leave. . . . If any one will not welcome you or listen to your words, shake off the dust from your feet as you leave that house or town. Truly I tell you, it will be more tolerable for the land of Sodom and Gomorrah on the day of judgment than for that town." (Matthew 10:5-15)

48

What is the reference in this gospel incident? There is no reference to sex. But there is a clear reference to rejection of God's messengers. The parallel between the gospel and Sodom is the closed heart that rejects the stranger, the wickedness that will not welcome God's heralds.

There are other less direct biblical references to Sodom: Isaiah 1:10-17 and 3:9, Jeremiah 23:14 and Zephaniah 2:8-11. The sins listed in those places are injustice, oppression, partiality, adultery, lies and encouraging evildoers.

Adultery is the only sexual sin in that list, and even in this case sex itself is not the concern. In the mind of the Hebrew Testament, adultery is not an offense against a woman nor against the intimacy of marriage nor against the inherent requirements of sex. Adultery is an offense against justice. Adultery offends the man to whom the women belongs. Adultery is the misuse of another man's property.

The Bible often uses Sodom as an example of the worst sinfulness, but the concern is never simply sexual acts. Oh, how small-minded that would be! Least of all is the concern homogenital acts.

The Sin of Sodom Today

Even Jesus understood the sin of Sodom as the sin of inhospitality. Other passages in the Bible come right out and say the same thing. Yet people continue to cite the story of Sodom to condemn gay and lesbian people.

There is a sad irony about the story of Sodom when understood in its own historical setting. People oppose and abuse homosexual men and women for being different, odd, strange or, as they say, "queer." Lesbian women and gay men are just not allowed to fit in. They are made to be outsiders, foreigners in our society. They are disowned by their families, separated from their children, fired from their jobs, evicted from apartments and neighborhoods, insulted by public figures, denounced from the pulpit, vilified on religious radio and TV, and then beaten in the schools and killed on the streets and in the backwoods of our nation. All this is done in the name of religion and supposed Judeo-Christian morality.

Such wickedness is the very sin of which the people of Sodom were guilty. Such cruelty is what the Bible truly condemns over and over again.

49

So those who oppress homosexuals because of the supposed "sin of Sodom" may themselves be the real "sodomites," as the Bible understands it.

Four. The Abomination of Leviticus: Uncleanness

The specific concern in the story of Sodom is not sex acts. But there is one reference in the Hebrew Testament where male-male sex is the concern. Leviticus 18:22 states, "You shall not lie with a male as with a woman; it is an abomination." Then Leviticus 20:13, completing this reference, adds the punishment: "If a man lies with a male as with a woman, both of them have committed an abomination; they shall be put to death, their blood is upon them."

In this passage the Bible uses a roundabout way of talking: to lie with a male as with a woman. The Hebrew text, translated literally, is even more obscure. It reads, "With a male you shall not lie the lyings of a woman." Obviously, "lying the lyings" refers to lying down or "going to bed" to have sex. There is no doubt that the text refers to male homogenital acts, but there is no hint of lesbian sex here. The offense is called an abomination, and the prescribed penalty is death. This all sounds pretty straightforward, and it sounds pretty bad. But what does this text mean in its own time and place?

They Shall be Put to Death

First, consider the death penalty. It really is severe. But Leviticus prescribes the same penalty for cursing one's parents. Other sexual sins also merit the death penalty: adultery, incest and bestiality. The law in Leviticus considered all these crimes to be very serious—but for different reasons.

Cursing one's parents was a major crime against society. Israelite society of the time was built around the extended family, the clan or the tribe. Slaves were subject to the children of the household. The children in turn were subject to their parents, and the mother was subject to her husband. Yet even the husband remained subject to his own father, as long as his father was alive. The eldest father and husband, the patriarch, was head of the whole household, which included people, animals, land and other property. The patriarch might be something like the mayor of a town in our system of government. The operation of that whole patriarchal system depended on obedience within the family hierarchy. So to oppose one's parents was to threaten social disorder. In our terms such behavior would be insurrection or treason, punishable by death. The laws of patriarchal China also imposed decapitation as the penalty for striking one's father

Adultery was another matter. For us, a married person, man or woman, commits adultery by having sex outside of the marriage. The offense is infidelity, betrayal of a trust or commitment, and it is against one's husband or wife. It is a personal offense. In ancient Israel, adultery was an offense only against the husband; it was an unlawful use of his property—his woman, his wife. More than a personal offense, it involved a financial loss: the man had paid his wife's father a bridal price for her, and her ability to bear children was important to the expansion of his family, the increase of his property.

Marriage and childbearing determined lines of ownership and inheritance in the patriarchal family. Property was passed on to the male children. Unlike the Romans, the Israelites did not recognize adoption as a basis for inheritance. It was important that the child born of a man's woman be his legitimate heir. But if someone else had sex with a man's wife and she later had a child, whose child would it be? To what property would the child be entitled? Similarly, if a man's new bride was not a virgin, how sure could he be that a child born through her was his own? A "used" woman was of no value to anyone.

Having sex with someone else's woman could cause serious financial and social problems. The "theft" involved was major. In ancient Israel, that offense was serious enough to be punished by death.

So merely knowing that a certain crime carried the death penalty does not say very much. One needs to ask, What really was the offense being punished? Why was the offense so serious? Was the death penalty carried out in practice? Cursing one's parents and committing adultery meant very different things in ancient Israel than they do in our culture.

Similarly, engaging in homogenital acts had a very different meaning. As we will see below, that two men shared a sexual experience was really not a problem. The only problem was when one man penetrated another. Among the early Israelites, as Leviticus sees it, to engage specifically in male-male intercourse was to mix the roles of man and woman. Such "mixing of kinds" was an abomination; it was impure–like sowing two different kinds of seed in a field or making cloth from both cotton and linen. In a primitive and superstitious way of thinking, the impurity of this sexual offense was serious enough to possibly defile the whole land. Israel was concerned not to lose the territory that it had struggled so hard to possess. Defile the land and you might lose it. Losing the land because of uncleanness among the people was too much to risk. The penalty for such risky behavior had to be severe. Like a broken seal on a sterile medicine, one unclean act could defile the whole people. The flaw must be corrected. The betrayer must be eliminated. The land must be preserved. Hence, the death penalty. But such thinking has nothing to do with male-male sex today.

A Religious Consideration: Jewish Differentness

The condemnation of homogenital acts occurs in a section of Leviticus called "The Holiness Code." This list of laws and punishments spells out requirements for Israel to remain "holy" in God's sight. But what does this word *holy* mean?

According to Jewish belief, Israel was God's "chosen people." Israel was bound to God by a covenant, a pact. That covenant required that the Israelites show themselves different from the other nations. They were God's People. They were to maintain their own traditions. They were not to do things the way the other nations did. They needed to preserve their religious identity. "With God's help" they had conquered the Canaanites and had taken over the Canaanite territory as their own "promised land." They now were to have nothing to do with the Gentiles. To remain separate from the Gentiles was to be "holy"—set apart, different, chosen, special, consecrated. They were to be like God, who is awesome, different, set apart. Differentness or specialness is the core meaning of holiness in the ancient Hebrew understanding.

So a main concern of The Holiness Code was to keep Israel different from the Gentiles. Thus, chapter 18 of Leviticus begins, "You shall not do as they do in the land of Egypt, where you lived, and you shall not do as they do in the land of Canaan, to which I am bringing you. You shall not follow their statutes. My ordinances you shall observe and my statutes you shall keep, following them: I am the Lord your God."

The Canaanite religion included fertility rites—or at least, that is how the Hebrew Testament portrays the matter. These ceremonies allegedly involved sexual rituals that were thought to bring blessing on the cycle of the seasons, the production of crops, the birth of livestock. Supposedly, during these rituals whole families and groups of families—husbands, wives, mothers, fathers, sons, daughters, aunts, uncles, brothers, sisters, cousins—all might have sex with one another.

Having sex with a menstruating woman and offering child-sacrifice to the Canaanite god, Molech, are other alleged Canaanite practices listed in this section of The Holiness Code.

The Holiness Code prohibits all those acts. It calls them all "abominations" and prescribes that "whoever commits any of these abominations shall be cut off from their people" (Leviticus 18:29). This same section of The Holiness Code includes the prohibition of male homogenital acts.

The point is that The Holiness Code of Leviticus prohibits male same-sex acts for religious reasons, not for sexual reasons. The concern is to keep Israel distinct from the Gentiles. Homogenital sex is forbidden because it is associated with Gentile identity. It departs from the Jewish understanding of how things should be.

The prohibition of male-male sex occurs only in The Holiness Code of Leviticus and nowhere else. But other prohibitions in The Holiness Code recur in other places in the Bible. Adultery is mentioned in Leviticus 18:20 and 20:10 and again in Exodus 20:14, Numbers 5:11-31, and Deuteronomy 5:18 and 22:22-27. Incest is mentioned in Leviticus 18:6-18 and 20:11-12, 14, 17, and 19-21, and again in Deuteronomy 22:30, 27:20, and 22-23. And bestiality is mentioned in Leviticus 18:23 and 20:15-16 and then also in Exodus 22:18 and Deuteronomy 27:21. These other offenses are forbidden in various contexts, but male-male sex is mentioned only in The Holiness Code. The implication is that the only reason for forbidding male-male sex is concern about uncleanness and holiness.

The argument in Leviticus is religious, not ethical or moral. That is to say, no thought is given to whether the sex in itself is right or wrong. The intent is to keep Jewish identity strong. The concern is purity.

Comparisons with Contemporary Experience

There used to be a church law that forbade Roman Catholics from eating meat on Fridays, and in some places the same requirement, now less strictly interpreted, still applies during Lent. That church law was considered so serious that violation was a mortal sin, supposedly punishable by hell. Yet no one believed that eating meat was something wrong in itself. The offense was against a religious responsibility: one was to act like a Catholic.

Or again, we sometimes hear of satanic rituals that include sexual acts. Jews and Christians today would certainly object to such sex. They would object even if the sex occurred between a married man and woman. Why? Not because a husband and wife have no right to share a sexual experience, but because that sex involves worship of the devil. Religious concerns, not sexual ethical ones, are the reason for the objection.

Those examples are parallels to the prohibition of male-male sex in Leviticus. Not sex, but violation of Judaism is what was prohibited.

The situation in ancient Israel was very different from our own. Except under unusual circumstances, sex in our culture has no implications for religious identity. No sex today, gay or straight, has the religious associations to which Leviticus objected. So the Leviticus code is irrelevant for deciding whether gay sex is right or wrong. Though the Hebrew Testament certainly did forbid penetrative male-male sex, its reasons for forbidding it have no bearing on today's discussion of homosexuality.

The ancient Jewish prohibition of male-male penetrative sex occurs in The Holiness Code. The point is this: the religious concern was purity and not the rightness or wrongness of the sex in itself. Now, two other considerations support this same conclusion. Consider what the Bible means by "abomination" and by "the lyings of a woman" and you will realize that Leviticus 18:22 was not referring to what we call "homosexuality" at all.

What is an Abomination?

The Leviticus text says that it is an "abomination" for a man to lie with a man as with a woman. In standard English, this sounds pretty bad. As one preacher vividly described it, an abomination is something that makes God want to vomit. But what does the word mean to the ancient Hebrew mind? There it's not as bad as it sounds to us.

Leviticus 20:25-26 captures the meaning of "abomination." It reads:

> You shall therefore make a distinction between the clean animal and the unclean, and between the unclean bird and the clean; you shall not bring abomination on yourselves by animal or by bird or by anything with which the ground teems, which I have set apart for you to hold unclean. You shall be holy to me; for I the Lord am holy, and have separated you from the peoples to be mine.

Evidently, "abominable" is just another word for "unclean." An "abomination" is a violation of the purity rules that governed Israelite society and kept the Israelites different from the other peoples.

Certain animals were thought to be clean and so allowed to be eaten; and for differing reasons certain other animals—like pigs, camels, lobsters and shrimp—were thought to be unclean, not to be eaten. Likewise, certain practices that involved the mixing of kinds—like sowing a field with two different kinds of seeds or weaving a cloth from two different kinds of fibers (Leviticus 19:19; Deuteronomy 22:11) or a man's having with another man the kind of sex a man has with a woman—were thought to be unclean and so were not to be done. Moreover, certain events, generally unavoidable—like menstruation in a women (Leviticus 15:19), seminal emission in a man (Leviticus 15:16: Deuteronomy 23:11), attending to a burial (Numbers 19:11), giving birth (Leviticus 12:2-5)–made a person unclean for a certain length of time.

It is difficult to recapture the meaning of "clean" and "unclean," "pure" and "impure," in ancient Israel. What was the rationale behind all those different instances of uncleanness? What made all those things abominations?

Some suggest that the Jewish purity rules were principles of sanitation and that certain things were forbidden because they were health hazards. Of course, some kind of health concerns and instances of spontaneous abhorrence were probably behind some of the purity rules. But the suggestion that the concern was hygiene presumes more medical knowledge than the ancients had, and the suggestion does not make complete sense of the purity laws. What is unhealthy about mixing cotton and linen in a fabric? Or cotton and polyester, for that matter?

Even in obvious matters of health, that suggestion does not pan out. For example, a person with certain skin diseases was considered "leprous"—not in today's technical sense of the term—and was declared unclean. But if the disease spread and covered the whole body, the person was no longer unclean: "since it has all turned white, he is clean" (Leviticus 13:13). Apparently, rather than disease or infection itself, completeness, wholeness or consistency is a key to Israel's notion of purity. But what sense does this make compared with what we now know about health and infection?

The ancient Israelites had their own conception about how things should be. They believed that certain rules of consistency or perfection governed God's creation. Fish should have fins and scales (Leviticus 11:9-12; Deuteronomy 14:9-10), so lobsters and shrimp are peculiar. They do not fit their aquatic kind, so they are off limits for human use. They are unclean. Similarly, land animals that have cleft hooves must also chew the cud (Leviticus 11:3-7: Deuteronomy 14:3-8). But pigs and camels do not meet these criteria. Pigs have cleft hoofs but do not chew the cud, and camels chew the cud but do not have cleft hoofs. There must be something amiss about them, so they are forbidden, taboo. And birds, it seems, were supposed to eat fruits and grains, not meat. So carnivorous birds are imperfect and thus impure (Leviticus 11:14-19; Deuteronomy 14:11-20).

These conceptions may seem like sheer superstition to us, but that is the way the ancient Israelites thought. And we are not so different. We have our own superstitions—about walking under a ladder or picking a lottery ticket or numbering a floor in a building "13." All peoples, primitive and contemporary, have their peculiar ways of understanding the world, and while we take our own for granted, we find the worldview of others weird.

We do not fully understand the ancient Jewish worldview. The reasons for the purity laws of Leviticus are lost in history and in layer upon layer of editing that gave us the text we now have. In addition to concerns about consistency in the natural world, religious considerations probably also played a part. Some animals were associated with pagan religious rituals, magic and superstition. The pig, for example, was used in Babylonian worship of the god Tammuz. This religious connection might be another reason for the Jews to consider the pig taboo.

The ancient Hebrew mind also had very particular ideas about man and woman. Woman is to be penetrated, and man is to penetrate. The very Hebrew word for woman, *naqeba*, means "orifice bearer"–as if there were no orifices in the male body. The fundamental image of a woman was someone who was there to serve the man in sexual intercourse. So for a man to sexually penetrate another man in anal intercourse was to mix and confuse the standards of maleness and femaleness. It was to use a male in the function of a female. It was precisely this mixing of kinds, this confusion of accepted gender roles, that Leviticus 18:22 forbade—but not other kinds of male-male sex. In the ancient Hebrew mind, penetrative sex with another man disrupted the ideal order of things and thus was unclean, taboo, forbidden; it was an abomination.

Whatever the rationale was behind the ancient Hebrew purity laws, such thinking certainly has nothing to do with ethics as we understand it. Indeed, such thinking is almost completely foreign to our own culture.

The Lyings of a Woman

Still, that is the thinking behind the prohibition of Leviticus 18:22 and 20:13. A man was not to be penetrated, only a woman. Analysis of the phrase *the lyings of a woman* shows that this concern and only it was behind the taboo against male-male intercourse.

In addition to the "lyings of a woman," the Bible also uses the phrase *the lying of a man*. It occurs in Numbers 31:17, 18, and 35 and in Judges 21:11 and 12. A woman who has experienced the lying of a man—or who has "known man"—is no longer a virgin. This lying means sexual intercourse. The lyings of a woman and the lying of a man appear to be two sides of the same coin. When a woman experiences the lying of a man, the man simultaneously experiences the lying of a woman. The man offers sexual penetration to the woman, and the woman offers reception of penetration to the man. So the lying of a woman refers to the experience of sexual penetration.

The "lyings" are plural in the case of a woman. Why? Because the ancients were fully aware that there were two possible kinds of lying with a woman: one could have vaginal sex as well as anal sex. And according to rabbinical commentary on the Jewish Law, anal intercourse with a man other than one's husband also qualified as adultery. Through and through, the concern is about sexual penetration. So when Leviticus 18:22 says that a man is not to lie the lyings of a woman with another man, it is specifically forbidding penetrative sex with a man.

It has often been noted that Leviticus forbids sex between two men but says nothing about sex between women. Why is this? One common answer is that women were of little importance in ancient patriarchal society. There was no reason to mention women. They did not matter.

But this reason does not hold up. The Bible is very concerned about women in other cases, and the Bible mentions women right alongside men when there is a question of blurring boundaries and mixing kinds. For example, for both males and females Deuteronomy 22:5 forbids cross-dressing. And the verse right after the prohibition of male-male sex, Leviticus 18:23, forbids both men and women from having sex with animals. The Bible really is concerned about women's behavior and forbids them from confusing male and female or mixing human and beast.

Then, why did the Bible not also forbid women from having sex with women? The answer is simply that sex between women would not count as sex. Real sex means penetration, and women just cannot do that with one another. When women have sex together, there is no risk of their blurring the lines between the penetrating function of a male and the receptive function of a female. No penetration occurs.

When President Bill Clinton was defending himself in his sex scandal, he claimed that he did not have sex with Monica Lowinsky. Later he clarified what he meant: he had not had sexual intercourse with her. The suggestion was that only intercourse counts as real sex. Many people laughed at this defense and said it was splitting hairs. Certainly, in our society the word *sex* generally does refer to more things than intercourse. Yet Clinton's defense squared perfectly with the mentality of the Hebrew Scriptures where only penetrative sex really counts.

And that idea is not totally foreign to our society. Researchers who were concerned about the spread of AIDS found that they had to be very careful about how they worded their questionnaires. When they asked people simply if they had sex, they often got the answer, No. But in conversation it became clear that these people had indeed engaged in all kinds of sex that could transmit HIV. But since the sex acts were not intercourse, people said they were not having sex. The researchers quickly began to specify the sex acts on their questionnaires.

Behind the prohibition of Leviticus 18:22 lay the notion that only penetrative sex counts. What was forbidden was "real sex" between men, anal penetration. Other sex acts between men and sex between women simply did not fall under the prohibition. Being non-penetrative, other sex acts did not blur the idealized line between female and male, so other sex acts were not considered impure, they were not abominations.

In the second to fifth centuries, C.E. (it is hard to date these sources precisely), Jewish rabbis discussed Leviticus and understood its rules in precisely this way. For example, when they spoke of male Gentile converts who had sex with young men—"sporting with boys," they called it—the rabbis were very clear that Leviticus forbade only anal intercourse. They considered other sexual activity a form a masturbation, which was discouraged but not forbidden. Similarly, when the rabbis discussed sex between women, "rubbing," they were clear that such sex did not violate a woman's virginity and was not forbidden. Likewise, they even considered the case of a woman sleeping with her male child and the possibility of their "rubbing." Only if the boy's penis entered the woman's vagina was this a matter of concern. And discussion of male-male friendship left room for profound intimacy, which may well have also included sexual contact but, of course, not penetration.

Early Jewish thinking had rather liberal ideas about sex, certainly when compared to our own. Perhaps most peculiar of all, categorizing acts as same-sex versus opposite-sex just did not enter the picture. The notions of homosexuality and heterosexuality are foreign to the biblical mind. What mattered was not with whom one had sex, male or female, but what one did: whether it was penetrative or not. Sexual penetration was reserved as a male-female thing. For a man to penetrate another man was a mixing of kinds. Such mixing was abomination, a religious impurity. Concern was not at all about homosexuality; such thinking was simply absent. Concern was about purity rules. These served to maintain an ideal order of things according to the ancient Jewish conception of the world.

This same conclusion applies to transvestism and transsexualism. The only relevant Bible quote would be Deuteronomy 22:5, which forbids cross-dressing. It forbids cross-dressing as an abomination, a religious taboo, and not as something unethical or wrong in itself. The prohibition is based on that peculiar ancient Jewish understanding of the ideal order of the universe. The prohibition has nothing to do with questions of homosexuality, transvestism, and transsexualism, as we have come to understand these complex psychosocial matters today. Obviously, then, the Bible offers no moral teaching about these things. The Bible does not address these questions. It speaks only about religious taboos in ancient Israel.

Contemporary Examples of Uncleanness

Leviticus prohibited penetrative male-male sex, and only this; and it prohibited it as an uncleanness, and only this. It was thought to violate an idealized conception of the universe. Of course, it is hard for us to understand this thinking. The ancient Jewish world was very different from ours. Rules of ritual purity do not feature large in our culture.

This is not to say that there is no concern for "clean" and "unclean" in our own day. We still do sometimes call things "dirty," and we mean disgusting and forbidden, just as the ancient Israelites did. But our reasoning is different. And even among ourselves, there is hardly anything that everyone would agree is "dirty" or "unclean." The following examples may at least provide a comparison with Israel's concern about cleanness and uncleanness.

Except for mixing up God in the matter, the preacher was on target when he said that an abomination, something dirty, makes you "want to vomit." What a culture considers dirty is usually something that makes its members uncomfortable. They feel funny, perhaps even feel sick. We learn what's "dirty" when we're little and people say, "Ugh! That's dirty!" "That's gross!" We learn to feel uncomfortable about things that the people around us don't like—like throwing food or soiling our pants or playing in the potty. Being "dirty" does involve uncomfortable feelings—and those feelings are learned.

Perhaps most people would agree that picking your nose and eating snot is gross and disgusting. Some might even say it's dirty, especially when talking to a child.

But just because it's dirty, just because people find it disgusting, does not mean it is wrong. In fact, eating snot is not even unhealthy. Mucus that is not removed from the nose just passes down the back of the throat and into the stomach anyway. Dirty and wrong do not necessarily go together—neither in our culture nor in ancient Israel.

In some societies people eat dogs, cats, snails, raw fish, ants or grasshoppers. To us that may be disgusting. It may seem gross or dirty. But it certainly is not wrong. It is just something with which *we* are uncomfortable.

In the early 1950s, styles were changing and women were just beginning to wear pants suits. Lots of women felt uncomfortable about that and even debated whether or not it was right. Should women wear pants outside the home or for shopping or even in church? From childhood they were taught how girls are supposed to dress. Though it was only custom they learned, they had never known anything else. Their custom seemed eternal decree, "the way it has always been." Some even argued, "God never meant for women to wear pants!" Custom was turned into the law of God. A matter of mere social convention was thought to be a matter of morality.

That same kind of thinking surrounded other issues as the styles changed: women smoking or driving cars, men wearing long hair or brightly colored shirts or earrings and other jewelry. What felt uncomfortable was taken to be wrong. Social taboo was turned into sin. Today most of these things are taken for granted, but as regards smoking, the tide has changed again. What had become chic is now often considered offensive. And this time, for solid ethical reasons, serious health concerns, smoking is again said to be wrong and sinful.

That same uncomfortable feeling and descriptions like "disgusting" and "gross" often also surround sexual matters. But sex may be the one topic for which we still use the words "dirty" or "impure."

Supposedly, certain sexual words are dirty, and they really upset some people. But other people just shrug all this off. With more frequent usage, the emotional impact of "dirty words" has worn off.

Similarly, many people are uncomfortable with sex, so children "pick up" from them that sex is "dirty." Many people never get beyond the influence of those powerful feelings, learned early in life. They never appreciate the difference between what is supposed to be dirty and what is wrong. Especially where sex is concerned, for them "wrong" means that they feel funny about it.

Most people's attitude toward homosexuality is just like that. They feel funny about it, so they say it's wrong. Pressed to explain why it's wrong, they cannot come up with good reasons. They just squirm and screw up their face, seeming to say, "It disgusts me" or "I just don't like it." But "dirty" has to do with custom and feelings, not with reasoned ethical judgments. And so it is, too, with the prohibition of male-male anal sex in Leviticus.

The book of Leviticus calls male-male intercourse an abomination. The early Israelites considered it unclean. They thought it was dirty. They prohibited it not because it was thought wrong in itself but because it offended their religious worldview.

All things supposedly fit into an idealized world order, and what did not was thought strange and offensive—unclean, abominable. When sex is defined in terms only of penetration, male-male intercourse makes a man function as a woman. Such confusion of functions disturbs the idealized order of creation. To God's "chosen people," set apart from the others, required to maintain their distinctive ways, this act was intolerable, it was a religious offense. So for religious reasons, as a requirement of Jewish identity, it was forbidden. Its being forbidden had nothing to do with the nature of sex *per se* nor with the bare fact that it was sex between two men.

A Hebrew and Greek Word Study

The very Hebrew term used in Leviticus conveys the meaning just explained. "Abomination" is a translation of the word *toevah*. This term could also be translated "uncleanness" or "impurity" or "dirtiness." "Taboo," what is culturally or ritually forbidden, would be another accurate translation.

The significance of the term *toevah* becomes clear when you realize that another Hebrew term *zimah* could have been used—if that was what the authors intended. *Zimah* means, not what is objectionable for religious or cultural reasons, but what is wrong in itself. It means an injustice, a sin.

Clearly, then, Leviticus does not say that for man to lie with man is a sin. Leviticus says it is a ritual violation, an uncleanness; it is something "dirty."

The conclusion of this little word study is no accident. It finds further confirmation in the Septuagint, the ancient Greek translation of the Hebrew Testament.

In the centuries before Christ, more and more Jews were living outside of Palestine. Many of them no longer understood Hebrew, but they did speak Greek, the common language of the Roman Empire at that time. So sometime between 300 and 150 B.C.E., a Greek translation of the Hebrew Scriptures was prepared so that Greek-speaking Jews could still read and study their Sacred Scriptures.

In the Septuagint, the Hebrew word *toevah* in Leviticus 18:22 is translated with the Greek word *bdelygma*. This is the word most commonly used in the Old Testament to translate *toevah*. Fully consistent with the

Hebrew, the Greek *bdelygma* means a ritual offense. In other places, like Proverbs 3:22, 6:16, and 16:5, *toevah* is actually translated uncleanness, *akatharsia*. (This very Greek word plays an important role in the first chapter of Romans, as we shall see.)

But once again, there were other Greek words available—like *anomia*, which means a violation of law or a wrong or a sin; or *poneria*, evil practice; or *asebia*, ungodliness. These words could have been used to translate *toevah*. In fact, in some cases they were. In nine places in chapter 16 of Ezekial—where the prophet outright defines the sin of Sodom—*toevah* is translated as *anomia*, and the offenses in question are not just ritual impurity but real wrongs, like idolatry, child sacrifice, adultery and basic wickedness. *Anomia* also translates *toevah* in Ezekial 18:12, 13 and 24, where the discussion is about individual moral responsibility. In Proverbs 26:25, referring to a deceitful and wicked person, *poneria* is used to translate *toevah*. And in Ezekial 14:6, in reference to idolatry, the Greek work *asebia* is used to translate the Hebrew *toevah*.

The ancient Greek translators could also have used *anomia* or *poneria* or *asebia* to translate *toevah* in the case of "man lying with man." They could have used one of these stronger terms with clear ethical implications—if that is what they intended. They did not use an ethical term; they used *bdelygma*.

Evidently, the Jews of that pre-Christian era did not understand Leviticus to forbid male-male intercourse as something wrong in itself. They understood Leviticus to forbid male-male intercourse as an offense against Jewish religion: it violated their understanding of the ideal order of creation, so it was Gentile-like, it was unjewish, it was dirty. And that is exactly how they translated the Hebrew text into Greek centuries before Christ.

The Meaning of Leviticus 18:22

All the evidence points to the same conclusion:

- an analysis of The Holiness Code and its cultural context,
- the meaning of "abomination,"
- the meaning of the "lyings of a woman" and

• a study of the Hebrew and Greek terms used in the Leviticus text.

All the evidence shows that Leviticus 18:22 forbids male-male intercourse—and only this—because of its cultural and religious implications. But Leviticus makes no statement about the morality of homogenital acts as such or in general. These were evidently not a concern in the Hebrew Testament.

Therefore, it is a misuse of the Bible to quote Leviticus as an answer to today's ethical question, whether gay sex is right or wrong. Leviticus was not addressing this question. The concern in Leviticus, the cultural context of that text, and the meaning of male-male sex in ancient Israel are all very foreign to the present situation. Today's question and that in Leviticus are simply two different things. Leviticus was concerned about social and religious taboos; we are concerned about sexual ethics.

Well then, does the Bible offer some positive teaching in its treatment on homogenital acts in Leviticus?

Distilled through an historical-critical reading of the text, the biblical lesson is this: Appreciate the legitimate place of taboos in society.

There is a difference between good taste and bad taste, between social propriety and grossness, between decency and indecency, between courtesy and rudeness. Recognizing and respecting this difference is important.

We avoid some behaviors not because they are particularly wrong in themselves but simply because they offend people. Picking one's nose, burping, or passing gas are obvious examples—in *our* culture.

Saying "bad" words is another example. But in fact, no word is bad, though some words are vulgar or crude. Still, depending on the situation, every word can be used for good or for harm. If certain words are offensive to some people, it might be wrong to use them around those people—not because the words themselves are wrong but because offending people is wrong. What is taboo is not necessarily wrong; still, under certain circumstances it might be wrong to break a taboo.

This examination of homogenital acts in Leviticus provides a useful reminder. Rules of etiquette and courtesy and accepted social conventions are necessary for the harmonious functioning of society. Much of what we do or avoid in public depends on what is socially acceptable or unacceptable. To attend to this matter is part of being respectful of other people. And it is part of being a virtuous person—or, said religiously, part of being a good Jew or a good Christian or a good member of any religion or society.

On the other hand, social conventions and taboos are always shifting and changing. Indeed, when conventions are misguided, unreasonable or oppressive, they ought to be changed, and change in these matters often entails heated debate and outright conflict. For this very reason, the turn of the 21st Century is a time of unprecedented social upheaval, and much of it centers around gender issues and sexual mores. There is no doubt that widespread ignorance, winked-at prejudice and blatant injustice attend current conventions regarding homosexuality. These do need to be reversed and their effects, overcome. They are not mere matters of innocuous custom or preferred rules of etiquette and good taste. They are personally and socially destructive conventions.

The lesson for today from Leviticus is to recognize the difference between real wrong and mere taboo and to respect each as is appropriate. Though it is not always easy to know the difference, we must not be hardheaded and treat as an ethical issue what is simply a matter of convention. Rather, with openness, intelligence, reasoned judgment and goodwill, we must continually work together to form a just, high-minded and noble society.

Five. Purity Concerns in the Christian Testament

The Hebrew Testament forbids homogenitality for purity reasons. Male-male penetrative sex makes one unclean. It breaks a religious taboo. It oversteps the idealized line between male and female and violates the ancient Jews' peculiar conception of order in the universe. Thus, it blurs one's Jewish identify and makes one look like a Gentile. The Hebrew Scriptures also list other purity requirements—like washing at prescribed times or not eating certain foods.

The prime example of such a religious requirement in Judaism was the circumcision of all males. If a man was not circumcised, he did not qualify as a Jew. If he did not bear on his body the mark of the religion of Israel, he was not a member of God's chosen people.

But no one thought that God rejected the uncircumcised, that they could not be just and holy, that they could not enjoy God's approval. The prophets of Israel often praised the righteousness of Gentile people even while condemning Israelites for abandoning God's ways. Likewise, no one thought that non-Jews had to follow the dietary laws of the Jewish religion, though many Gentiles were recognized as good people. Circumcision and the purity requirements of the Jewish Law were part of being a Jew. They were not necessarily part of being a good person, just and righteous before God.

Jesus' Teaching about Purity

Jesus knew that difference. He is very clear that being a good person and keeping the requirements of the Jewish Law are not the same thing. He is also very clear that the only thing that matters is being a good person. One of the reasons that Jesus was killed was because he challenged the real importance of the Jewish Law.

"Listen and understand," he said.

> It is not what goes into the mouth that defiles a person, but it is what comes out of the mouth that defiles. . . . What comes out of the mouth proceeds from the heart, and this is what defiles. For out of the heart come evil intentions, murder, adultery, fornication, theft, false witness, slander. These are what defile a person, but to eat with unwashed hands does not defile. (Matthew 15:10, 18-20)

In that way Jesus rejected the importance of the Jewish purity laws. The only purity that mattered for Jesus was "purity of heart."

Being "Pure of Heart"

What does this "cleanness of heart" mean? Some people took it to mean you were not supposed to have "dirty thoughts." You were not supposed to be "impure" in your mind. Of course, "dirty" and "impure" referred to sex: you were not supposed to think about sexual things.

What a distortion of Jesus' teaching! Jesus was not preoccupied with sex. He was concerned about being a good person, about being good to the core.

Jesus objected to external religious show—fasting so others can see, praying in front of everybody, putting a lot of money into the collection so others will notice. Jesus said, "Beware of practicing your piety before others in order to be seen by them. . . . Whenever you pray, go into your room and shut the door and pray to your Father who is in secret" (Matthew 6:1, 6). Jesus praised the widow who was able to put only the smallest of coins into the collection. He praised her because she gave from her heart (Mark 12:42-44).

Jesus insisted that virtue must go as deep as the heart. So in Mark 7:6, Jesus quotes the prophet Isaiah against those concerned about ritual washings: "This people honors me with their lips, but their hearts are far from me." Or when Jesus teaches about forgiveness, he says you must forgive others "from your heart" (Matthew 18:35). Or when Jesus teaches about sexual offenses against others, he says, "Everyone who looks at a woman with lust has already committed adultery with her in his heart" (Matthew 5:28). Jesus is not impressed with externals. He looks into the heart.

In summary Jesus says, "Blessed are the pure in heart, for they shall see God" (Matthew 5:8). For Jesus the "pure in heart" will see God, not those who are merely pure or clean according to the practices of the Jewish Law. Being a good person—honest, loving, just, kind, merciful, peaceful—is what matters before God. The purity requirements of the Law are no longer significant.

Early Christian Attitude Toward Purity

The early followers of Jesus held that same attitude toward the purity requirements of the Jewish Law. Chapter 15 of Acts of the Apostles—as well as many other places—records the debate in the early church about circumcision. Some claimed, "Unless you are circumcised according to the custom of Moses, you cannot be saved" (Acts 15:1). But the council of apostles and elders decreed that circumcision was not necessary. Thus, the early Christian church rejected a central requirement of the Jewish Law.

Peter, the leader of the twelve apostles, had come to that same conclusion regarding clean and unclean animals. In a dream, Peter

saw the heaven opened, and something like a large sheet coming down, being lowered to the ground by its four corners. In it were all kinds of four-footed creatures and reptiles and birds of the air. Then he heard a voice saying, "Get up, Peter; kill and eat." But Peter said, "By no means, Lord; for I have never eaten anything that is profane or unclean." The voice said to him again, a second time, "What God has made clean, you must not call profane." (Acts 10:11-15)

Soon Peter realized the far-reaching implications of that revelation. He applied it to people, to the Gentiles, saying, "God has shown me that I should not call anyone profane or unclean" (Acts 10:28). Peter explained himself with the same reasoning that Jesus used: "I truly understand that God shows no partiality, but in every nation anyone who fears God and does what is right is acceptable to God" (Acts 10:34). What matters is not ritual purity, not keeping the requirements of the Jewish Law, but justice and virtue.

The apostle Paul also makes the same point over and over. He writes, "Circumcision is nothing, and uncircumcision is nothing; but obeying the commandments is everything" (1 Corinthians 7:19). Or again, "For in Christ Jesus neither circumcision nor uncircumcision counts for anything; the only thing that counts is faith working through love" (Galatians 5:6).

Echoing the teaching of Jesus, Paul says, "A person is a Jew who is one inwardly, and real circumcision is a matter of the heart—it is spiritual and not literal" (Romans 2:29). In this way Paul reinterprets what it means to be God's chosen people; it is a matter of the heart. He states boldly, "I know and am persuaded in the Lord Jesus that nothing is unclean in itself" (Romans 14:14).

That teaching summarizes a major theme in Paul's letter to the Romans. And, as we shall see, in order to make that very point, Paul mentions homogenital acts at the beginning of that letter.

Homogenitality in the Christian Testament

What does the Christian teaching about purity of heart say about homogenital acts? The single text in the Hebrew Scriptures that talks about homogenitality forbids it—but precisely because it is "unclean," not because it is wrong in itself. The Christian Scriptures insist that cleanness and uncleanness do not matter. Only whether you are doing good or evil matters.

Jesus and the Christian Testament reject the only biblical basis for condemning male-male sex. So we should expect no condemnation of homogenitality in the Christian Scriptures. Or if there is such a blanket condemnation, we should expect it to include some new reason for the condemnation. We should expect the Christian Scriptures to show that something about homogenitality or homosexuality in itself is wrong— that is, harmful, unkind, destructive, unloving, dishonest, unjust or some such thing. Or else we should expect same-sex acts to be condemned only when they do include such wrongs, only when the sexual expressions are abusive, hurtful, wanton or lewd, just as heterosexual acts would be forbidden for these same reasons.

How do those expectations square with what the Christian Testament actually says? Following an historical-critical reading, they square perfectly well. There is no condemnation of homogenital sex in and of itself in the Christian Testament—neither because of purity concerns nor other concerns. At the same time, the Christian Testament is concerned about outlawing the abuse and exploitation that might be part of same-sex acts. Analysis of the relevant texts supports these conclusions.

74

Six. The Unnatural in Romans: Socially Unacceptable

There is only one Christian Bible text that actually discusses homogenital acts at any length. It occurs in the first chapter of Saint Paul's Letter to the Romans. This is the famous text from which people get the notion that gay sex is "unnatural." This is also the text from which they argue that venereal diseases—and today, HIV disease and AIDS—are punishment for homogenital activity. This may also be the only Bible text that mentions lesbian sex. But considering to whom Paul is writing, how he is making his point, and to what end, all these conclusions seem to be wrong.

Without doubt, this passage from Romans is the most important statement of homosexuality in the Bible. It occurs in the Christian Testament, so unlike Leviticus, no one can dismiss it as part of the "Old" Testament. And it is long and detailed, so unlike the other two references in the Christian Testament, which will be discussed in Chapter Seven, no one can claim it is a mere passing comment. But precisely because this passage is long, it provides a lot of material for analysis, and more and more surely as the evidence mounts, this analysis shows that this text has been misunderstood. It does not condemn homogenital acts as wrong.

Here is the text of Romans 1:18-32. Only verse 27 is a clear reference to homogenital acts, male homogenital acts, though verse 26 is said to refer to lesbian sex. To understand these two verses, however, the rest of this long passage is required. At critical points, the original Greek words are noted in parentheses. Reference to these later on will help explain the meaning of this passage.

> [18]For the wrath of God is revealed from heaven against all ungodliness (*asebeia*) and wickedness (*adikia*) of those who by their wickedness suppress the truth. [19]For what can be known about God is plain to them, because God has shown it to them. [20]Ever since the creation of the world his eternal power and divine nature, invisible though they are, have been understood and seen through the things he has made. So they are without excuse; [21]for though they knew God, they did not honor him as God or give thanks to him, but they became futile in their thinking and their senseless minds were darkened. [22]Claiming to be wise, they became fools; [23]and they exchanged the glory of the immortal God for images resembling a mortal human being or birds or four-footed animals or reptiles.
>
> [24]Therefore God gave them up in the lusts of their hearts to impurity (*akatharsia*), to the degrading (*atimazesthai*) of their bodies among themselves, [25]because they exchanged the truth about God for a lie and worshipped and served the creature rather than the Creator, who is blessed forever! Amen.
>
> [26]For this reason God gave them up to degrading (*atimias*) passions. Their women exchanged natural (*physiken*) intercourse for unnatural (*para physin*), [27]and in the same way also the men, giving up natural (*physiken*) intercourse with women, were consumed with passion for one another. Men committed shameless (*aschemosyne*) acts with men and received in their own persons the due penalty for their error.
>
> [28]And since they did not see fit to acknowledge God, God gave them up to a base mind and to things that should not be done. [29]They were filled (*pepleromenous*) with every kind of wickedness (*adikia*), evil, covetousness, malice. Full of envy, murder, strife, deceit, craftiness, they are gossips, [30]slanderers, God-haters, insolent, haughty, boastful, inventors of evil, rebel-

lious toward parents, [31]foolish, faithless, heartless, ruthless. [32]They know God's decree, that those who do such things deserve to die—yet they not only do them but even applaud those who practice them.

This chapter summarizes the scholarly work of the late John Boswell and especially of L. William Countryman. This study of Romans 1:18-32 comes to a conclusion that is quite different from what is generally heard: far from condemning same-sex acts, Paul is actually teaching that they are ethically neutral. Like heterosexual acts, homosexual acts are neither right nor wrong in themselves. They can be used for good or for evil, but in themselves they are neither. There is nothing wrong with gay or lesbian sex simply because it is homogenital.

Three major considerations support this conclusion, and all three lock together in one coherent interpretation.

• First, **The Vocabulary Paul Uses** describes homogenital acts as "impure," subject to social disapproval, but not as ethically wrong.

• Second, **The Structure of the Passage** sorts out and separates the impurity or social disapproval of the homogenital acts, on the one hand, from real wrong or sin, on the other.

• Third, analysis of **The Overall Plan of the Letter to the Romans** shows why Paul mentions homogenital acts though he does not think they are wrong. His purpose is to teach that in Christ the purity concerns of the Old Law no longer matter and they should not be dividing the members of the Christian community.

The Vocabulary Paul Uses

The "Unnatural": Out of the Ordinary

In Romans 1:26-27, Paul uses three words to describe same-sex acts: unnatural, degrading, and shameless. First we consider at length the words translated as "unnatural."

Paul says men "gave up natural relations with women and were consumed with passion for one another." This is certainly a reference to homogenital acts. And the "women exchanged natural relations for unnatural." The Greek words translated as "unnatural" are *para physin*. What do these words mean?

Physis is the Greek word for nature. It is the root of the English word "physics," the study of the natural world. The adjectival form of the same word, *physikos*, occurs in the English word "physical." But as even English usage suggests, the word could be used in various senses.

What exactly did Paul mean when he used this word? This is not easy to say, but this much is clear: Paul did *not* use the word *nature* in our abstract sense of "Nature and the Laws of Nature." His usage was more concrete. For Paul, the "nature" of something was its particular character or kind. Consider some examples.

In Galatians 2:15, Paul speaks of those who are Jews by nature, and in Romans 2:27, he speaks of those who are Gentiles by nature (though the literal reference to the Gentiles reads "uncircumcision by nature"). It is difficult to make sense of this usage. Attempting to do so, the English translations in our Bibles omit any reference to nature and simply read "Jews by birth (*physei*)" and "those who are physically (*ek physeos*) uncircumcised," but the Greek word for nature occurs in both these passages. In Romans 2:14, Paul speaks of Gentiles who follow their own conscience and "do instinctively (*physei*) what the law requires," but the Greek text reads "by nature," and the implication is that these Gentiles act as is consistent with the kind of persons they are. In Galatians 4:8, Paul mentions "beings that by nature (*physei*) are not gods," and his reference is to the powers or "spirits" which supposedly govern the universe. Or again, in 1 Corinthians 11:14, Paul writes, "Does not nature (*physis*) itself teach you that if a man wears long hair, it is degrading to him?"

In all those cases, Paul uses the term "nature" to imply what is characteristic or peculiar in this or that situation. You would not expect a Jew not to be a Jew or the uncircumcised not to be uncircumcised. That is, you would not expect someone raised as a Jew to be ignorant of the Jewish Law, and you would not expect a Gentile to act like a Jew; that is not their "nature." According to the standard practice of Paul's day, you would not expect men to wear long hair; that is not what "nature" requires (though it is obvious that Paul refers to custom and that "nature," as we understand the word, has nothing to do with the length of a man's hair—unless he happens to be bald). Once you knew the true God of the universe, you would not believe the forces of this world are divine; that is not to be expected, for by their very "nature" they are otherwise.

For Paul, something is *natural* when it responds according to its own kind, when it is as it is expected to be. For Paul, the word *natural* does not mean "in accord with universal laws." Rather, *natural* refers to what is characteristic, consistent, ordinary, standard, expected and regular. When people acted as was expected and showed a certain consistency, they were acting naturally. When people did something surprising, something unusual, something beyond the routine, something out of character, they were acting unnaturally. That was the sense of the word *nature* in Paul's usage.

Next, the Greek word *para* usually means "beside," "more than," "over and above," "beyond." We retain this meaning in many English words. A paraprofessional is someone who is not trained in a particular field but who assists those working in that field. For example, "paralegal" refers to people who are not lawyers but who work with lawyers and other legal professionals.

In a handful of stock phrases, *para* can also mean "contrary to," so *para physin* could be translated "contrary to nature." But given Paul's own usage of these terms, the sense is not "in opposition to the laws of nature" but rather "unexpectedly" or "in an unusual way," what we might mean if we said: "Contrary to her nature, Jean got up and danced last night."

So what does it mean when Romans says that the "women exchanged natural relations for unnatural and the men likewise gave up natural relations with women and were consumed with passion for one another"? It means that these women and men were engaging in sexual practices that were not the ones people usually perform. The practices were beyond the regular, outside the ordinary, more than the usual, not the expected.

There is no implication whatever in those words that the practices were wrong or against God or contrary to the divine order of creation or in conflict with the universal nature of things. For Paul those words do not mean "unethical." According to Paul's usage, those words only say that the practices were different from what one would generally expect.

Rather than "unnatural," the words *para physin* in Romans would more accurately be translated as "atypical"—unusual, peculiar, out of the ordinary, uncharacteristic.

Even God Acts "Unnaturally"

A study of the Greek words suggests that there is no ethical condemnation in Paul's use of *para physin*. This conclusion seems certain. Why? Because there is further evidence on the matter, and that evidence is weighty.

In Romans 11:24, Paul uses those very same words to talk about God. Paul describes how God grafted the wild branch of the Gentiles into the cultivated olive tree that is the Jews. Now Jew and Gentile are one in Christ. But to graft a wild tree into a cultivated tree is not the ordinary thing to do. Usually one grafts a branch of a cultivated tree into the stock of a wild tree. In this way the cultivated tree benefits from the vigor of the wild tree. Still, God acted in reverse order.

In Paul's understanding of the words, God himself acted *para physin*. God did what was "unnatural," that is to say, atypical. God behaved in an unusual way.

Paul's point is that God is not bound by standard expectations. God goes beyond what culture and society prescribe. God's ways are not our ways. And especially in Christ, God has chosen to do a new thing.

Indeed, a major theme in Paul's writings is that in Christ, God has set up a new order. The old ways have passed away; new things are happening. Thus, Paul writes in Galatians 6:15, "Neither circumcision nor uncircumcision is anything; but a new creation is everything!" And in 2 Corinthians 5:16-17: "From now on, therefore, we regard no one from a human point of view.... If anyone is in Christ, there is a new creation: everything old has passed away; see, everything has become new." Paul insists that standard social distinctions and cultural categories no longer hold sway.

In Galatians 3:28, Paul shows how radical this thought is when he writes, "There is no longer Jew or Greek, there is no longer slave or free, there is no longer male and female; for all of you are one in Christ Jesus." Clearly, Paul's thought tends toward transcending all social differences. Paul was hardly wedded to the status quo.

Still, did Paul always walk his talk? Did his practice square with his theory? On the question of Jew and Greek, Yes. In this case Paul forcefully broke down all barriers and insisted on the full equality of Jews and Gentiles in Christ.

But in the case of slavery, Paul's record is mixed. He said that a slave who became a Christian should remain a slave. But then he also pointed out that the slave's master is also a slave to Christ (1 Corinthians 7:21-24). And although Paul sent the slave Onesimus back to his owner, Philemon, Paul begged Philemon to receive Onesimus no longer as a slave but as a dear brother. Paul was really suggesting that Philemon free Onesimus.

The strong endorsements of slavery that do occur in the Christian Testament cannot be attributed to Paul: Ephesians 6:5-9, Colossians 3:22-4:1, and 1 Timothy 6:1-2 (and of course not 1 Peter 2:18). Though these letters are Pauline in character, though they follow the "Pauline school," they are late writings and are not Paul's own. They exhibit a conservative tendency that was affecting the maturing churches. Second- and third-generation Christians began to structure the church as an institution that would fit into society at large. In the process, they toned down some of Paul's far-reaching vision. The enforcement of status-quo slavery is not Paul's.

Finally, on the matter of the male and the female, Paul's record is also mixed. As in the case of slavery, the apostle Paul gets a bad name because of views his more conservative followers held. According to 1 Corinthians 14:34-35, women are not to speak in church. But this passage is a post-Pauline interpolation. It is not from Paul himself. Its insistence on the Jewish Law is contrary to Paul's central teaching, and it contradicts 1 Corinthians 11:5, which presumes that women are to speak out in church. Probably the misogynist Pauline circle that wrote 1 Timothy 2:11-15 was also behind the editorial addition in 1 Corinthians.

However, in some cases Paul supports the social requirements about gender roles. For example, in Romans 7:2, he teaches that women are "under their husbands," and in 1 Corinthians 11:1-16, that the husband is head of the wife, that women should wear veils and cover their heads, and that men should not have long hair. Yet in this same passage he suggests that men are also dependent on women and that these requirements are in some way just customs. Moreover, Paul had women in positions of authority and power in the churches he founded. In the final chapter of the Letter to the Romans, among a total of 29 people, Paul mentions ten women. Three have important roles: Phoebe is a deacon, Prisca is a co-worker and leader of a house church, and Junia is counted among the apostles. This is powerful stuff.

If Paul did not fully succeed in balancing the roles of men and women, he was certainly moving in that direction. He was certainly open to the new creation about which he wrote. Paul was not alone in this matter, and he would not even have been breaking new ground. To advance the cause of women was not a new idea. Most obviously, Paul had the example of Jesus. Moreover, there were burgeoning "feminist" movements throughout the Roman Empire at that time. As part of a broader cultural movement, Paul was indeed challenging the expected roles of men and women in society.

So Paul's treatment of male and female gender roles is an exact parallel to his treatment of Jewish/Gentile relations. In both cases, Paul is pushing the envelope. In both cases he is challenging social distinctions. Therefore, when in Romans 11:24 Paul says that God acts in ways that are *para physin* as regards Jews and Gentiles, there is every reason to believe that Paul has the same meaning in mind in Romans 1:26 when he uses the same words *para physin* to describe matters of gender and sexual behaviors. The question of how Jews relate to Gentiles is a strictly Jewish concern. The Greek and Roman world had little interest in the matter. Yet in the middle of this typically Jewish discussion, Paul introduces a standard Greek phrase *para physin*. He uses technical Greek words to address an in-house Jewish question. How peculiar! Obviously, he is showing how he understands those Greek words and what he thinks of them when applied to Jewish and Christian questions. His point is that they have no moral or ethical relevance. "Unnatural"? Get real! God is not bound by social or cultural standards.

Used to describe God's actions, the words *para physin* must mean "atypical" and not "unnatural" or "immoral." If these words did mean "immoral," Paul would be saying that God is immoral, that God acts unethically. God would be working against the very principles of good and evil that God stands for. God would be fully whimsical, changing from one time to another, unexpectedly shifting the meaning of right and wrong. Such an idea is patently absurd. There can be no moral or ethical meaning in those Greek words for Paul.

Therefore, in the first chapter of Romans in reference to homogenital acts, the words *para physin* must similarly imply no moral condemnation. Rather, those words flag Paul's desire to move beyond the divisive sexual standards of his day. The conclusion stands firm: in the Letter to the Romans Paul is not teaching that same-sex acts are immoral.

Other Opinions about *para physin*

There is considerable debate on this matter. Some biblical scholars insist that *para physin* does mean "unnatural" or "contrary to nature" and understand "nature" in the abstract sense of "Nature and Nature's Laws." The term *para physin* was used in Stoic philosophy, which pervaded the Roman Empire in Paul's day, and by then Stoic philosophy was well on its way to developing a notion of natural law built into the universe.

We use the words "stoic" or "stoical" today to mean unfeeling, unmoved by emotion, austere, rigidly disciplined. This popular meaning comes from Stoic insistence that all things are governed by a law built into nature and that human reason can discern that law. Virtue consists in living by reason, not by emotions or feelings. One is to follow the laws of nature.

When applied to sex, this philosophy said that the purpose of sex is procreation, so any use of sex for mere pleasure violates its core nature. Thus, Stoicism is one important source of the sex-negativism that has pervaded Western civilization. Any non-procreative sex was called *para physin*. Homogenitality—and other sex acts, like heterosexual intercourse during the woman's period—fell into this category. Sex that could be procreative was called *kata physin* or "according to nature." Thus, when the world of Paul's day spoke of sex *para physin*, the reference might be homogenital acts.

Paul was certainly aware of that terminology. He could hardly have lived in the Greek-speaking world of his day without picking up some Stoic thought. Indeed, in the very passage of Romans under consideration here, Paul speaks of "things that should not be done" (1:28). The Greek is *ta me kathekonta*, and this is another standard Stoic formula.

And in that first chapter of Romans, there are other words commonly used in Stoic philosophy.

Some biblical scholars go so far as to suggest that in this passage Paul integrates Stoic thought about natural law with Jewish and Christian thought about God's creation of the world. For Paul refers to the Creator, and Paul faults the Gentiles for worshiping images of humans, birds, beasts and snakes. So these scholars conclude that Paul had in mind the Genesis account of creation of the world and of all the animals as well as the role of Adam and Eve, man and woman, as part of God's plan. They argue that Paul sees homosexuality as a violation of this plan, as the subversion of the natural order built into the created universe.

However, the more common opinion is that only Wisdom 13:1-9, and not Genesis, is behind Paul's argument in Romans 1:18-23. The theme in Wisdom closely parallels Paul's criticism of the Gentiles. They ought to know God from all that is created, but they foolishly worship idols instead. Moreover, to find a case about sexual orientation in Genesis is clearly to read into that ancient text a concern from our own day. In no way was Genesis dealing with sexual orientation. More on this in Chapter Eight.

The key question in this debate is whether to read Paul on his own terms or in terms of Stoic philosophy. Though Paul certainly knew some technical Stoic terms and even uses them in this section of Romans, close attention to how Paul uses them suggests he ignores their technical meaning—if he even understood it.

Clearly, Paul does not use the term "nature" the way the Stoics did. Paul's usage is concrete; the Stoic usage is abstract. Moreover, although Paul is aware that sex *para physin* would refer to non-procreative sex, including same-sex acts, he certainly is not concerned about procreation. Paul was expecting the speedy return of Christ, the end of the world, so nowhere in his writings does he show concern for procreation.

Finally, in Romans 11:24, Paul seems to take the technical Stoic terminology and throw it to the wind. Paul uses the analogy of grafting cuttings into a stock. He writes to the Gentiles about the Jews as follows: "God has the power to graft them in again. For if you have been cut from what is by nature [*kata physin*] a wild olive tree and grafted, contrary to nature [*para physin*], into a cultivated olive tree, how much more will these natural [*kata physin*] branches be grafted back into their own olive tree." Paul seems deliberately to play with the Stoic terms *kata physin* and *para physin*. And in their technical sense he mangles them. In Paul's mind, it seems, to speak of "natural" or "unnatural" in the face of God is to speak foolishly. These prescriptions have no hold on the power and mercy of God.

Do not miss the point. It is not that Paul is opting for a miraculous, rather than a down-to-earth approach to religion. It is not that Paul is rejecting natural-law theory. The point is that Paul simply did not think in terms of natural law. If he did, he could not and would not have portrayed God acting "contrary to nature."

However, Paul's use of *para physin* is not at all unusual. Bernadette Brooten's recent research into ancient astrological texts, formulas for erotic spells, medical textbooks and handbooks on dream interpretation shows that, in addition to the technical meaning of the Stoic terms, there was also a popular understanding prevalent throughout the Roman Empire. Paul was not a Greek philosopher but a converted Jew and a Christian preacher. It is to be expected that he would use Stoic terminology in its popular, rather than its technical, sense.

This new research is striking. The popular meaning of *para physin*, just recently documented, squares perfectly with older conclusions about how Paul used these words, as just summarized. In the popular mind, natural meant what was culturally prevalent and socially accepted. In this sense, the ideas of nature and custom were virtually interchangeable— which is no surprise. Probably every society thinks that its standard practice is what is natural and that what other peoples do differently is weird, unnatural and even wrong. So when Paul used *para physin* in Romans 1:26 to mean atypical, he was following the everyday usage of his day.

When it came to sex, the standard Roman expectation was that men are active and women are passive, men penetrate and women are penetrated. Such behavior would be "natural." This thinking is similar to what we saw in the discussion of the ancient Jewish notions in Chapter Four—but there are important differences. The Jewish concern was purity, the Roman concern was social status.

In the ancient Jewish mind, an idealized boundary between the male and the female was the rule. So sex between women hardly mattered, because it was non-penetrative. And penetrative sex between men, all men, any male with any male, was taboo, unclean, abominable, because it blurred the idealized line between the male and the female. In contrast, in the Roman mind, there was a pecking order; a hierarchy of social status was the rule. Adult male citizens could have penetrative sex with women and with male and female noncitizens, slaves, and youth. Male-male sex was fully accepted, except for this restriction: adult male citizens were generally not to have penetrative sex with one another nor be penetrated by anyone else. Such sex would disrupt the pecking order. In the Roman world, women were also subject to the pecking order, completely so. They were not to have sex without a man; they were to be passive and receptive of male penetration. To act otherwise would be "unnatural"—that is, counter-cultural.

Those were the mixed social expectations that Paul was addressing when he spoke of "unnatural" sex in Romans 1. The question is this, Did Paul understand these social expectations as also morally binding? When he spoke of what was *para physin*, did he think the atypical or "unnatural" was also unethical?

The answer proposed here is definitely, "No." When Paul wrote that the women and the men were doing sexually "unnatural" things, he was referring to customs and social norms, and he was aware of how varied they were. He was not suggesting that they are ethically binding but, on the contrary, that in Christ such cultural considerations are ethically irrelevant. Deviations from the norm are merely atypical. God's way transcends cultures and societies. God does the unusual. God acts *para physin*. In Christ a new order has emerged. Typical or atypical, socially accepted or socially forbidden, *kata physin* or *para physin*—these notions have no moral weight.

A list of other considerations unfolds below and confirms this same conclusion. Paul's Christian mind on this matter is very different from what technical and popular Stoic terminology, Jewish purity rules or the opinions of his day would suggest. The visionary Paul must be read on his own terms and not as an echo of the surrounding culture.

What about Lesbian Sex?

The words *para physin* actually occur in verse 26. It talks about women who "exchanged natural intercourse for *unnatural*." Is this a reference to female same-sex acts? Many have thought so.

One reason people think verse 26 refers to lesbian sex is because it mentions "unnatural" sexual relations, and, as the term is used today, *unnatural* sex means homogenital acts. But this reasoning is not worth considering. It ignores the fact that terms shift meaning throughout the centuries.

A more serious reason is that in Paul's day the Stoic term *para physin* could apply to homogenital acts. Stoicism held that sex was for procreation, so any non-procreative use was "contrary to nature" and considered morally wrong.

But, as we have seen, Paul did not use the words *para physin* in the technical Stoic sense. Even if Paul knew those words could be used to refer to same-sex acts, the implication of these words for him was not the same as for the Stoics. Paul used these words in the popular sense that simply meant atypical or outside the ordinary.

So Paul's reference to female sexual relations that are "beyond the ordinary" could mean many things. It might mean sex during menstruation, sex with an uncircumcised man, oral sex, heterosexual anal sex, having sex while standing up, or anything that would not be considered the standard way of having sex. In our own day, for example, some people would consider anything except the "missionary position" out of the ordinary. There is no need to read homogenitality into the p*ara physin* of verse 26. A figure as important, sex-negative and homophobic as Saint Augustine did not think Romans 1:26 referred to lesbian sex. And there is ongoing discussion among scholars today on this very point.

There is still another reason people might think verse 26 refers to female same-sex acts. The word *likewise* or *in the same way* links verse 26 with verse 27, and verse 27 clearly refers to male same-sex acts. That *in the same way* sets up a parallel between what the women do and what the men do.

But is the parallel that both the women and the men perform same-sex acts? Or is the parallel simply that both the women and the men gave up the expected way of having sex for something else, whatever it might be?

The latter explanation makes perfectly good sense of the text. The men and the women could both be involved in something atypical without both being involved in homogenitality.

In fact, if verse 26 refers to lesbianism, some explanation is needed. Lesbianism is not mentioned anywhere else in the Hebrew or the Christian Testaments. Why would Paul have brought up that subject and made an issue of it here? Why, if it is so important, is it never mentioned again?

And most important of all, how could lesbianism be included under the topic of Romans 1:24-27 that Paul had introduced? In verse 24, Paul specifically says that he is talking about impurity. He means ritual violation of the Jewish Law, which we discussed in Chapters Four and Five. Under this topic Paul mentions what the women do and then what the men do. The announced topic is impurity. But the Hebrew Scriptures never forbid female homogenitality. Later rabbinical discussion about the Jewish Law is rather unconcerned about female-female "rubbing." How could lesbian sex fall under the Jewish heading of impurity? Other things—like sex during the menstrual period or sex with an uncircumcised man or sex with animals—could have qualified as violating the Jewish Law. Paul may well have had something like that in mind when he spoke of the women doing sexual things *para physin* or outside the ordinary.

Only one Greek-language Jewish source is known to take up the issue of lesbianism and condemn it—*The Sentences of Pseudo-Phokylides*, dated somewhere between 30 B.C.E. and 40 C.E., and probably of Alexandrian origin. But this one piece of documented evidence is not reason enough to suppose that the whole Jewish world was now concerned about lesbianism and so was Paul when he wrote of atypical sex.

Still, in *Love Between Women*, Bernadette Brooten has argued powerfully that that is precisely what Paul had in mind. She shows that, in the Roman world at large, talk of "unnatural" sex in the case of women was commonly understood to refer to lesbianism. It was unnatural because it violated the accepted gender roles: in sex a woman was to be subordinate to, and penetrated by a man. Moreover, challenging the common line that we know virtually nothing about female-female sex in the classical world, Brooten amasses evidence for considerable awareness of lesbianism in the more popular writings of the day—formulas for erotic spells that were to bind lovers to one another, textbooks on astrology that explain how the stars determine people's sexual interests, medical treatments geared to "cure" women of same-sex desire, and a handbook on dream interpretation that exemplifies the inequality built into the sex roles of that ancient time.

Brooten's argument is that awareness of lesbianism was commonplace throughout the Roman Empire of Paul's day. So the average listener would take Paul's words, about women exchanging "natural intercourse for unnatural," to refer to lesbianism. And supposedly, this is precisely what Paul had in mind.

But who can say? As we have seen, Paul advocated and was working toward equality for women and men. He would not have simply bought into the gender norms of the Roman Empire and on this basis, lockstep with his culture, condemned sex between women as unnatural. Paul's vision was broader than that. Besides, from the Jewish perspective, his topic in that section of his letter is impurity, and lesbianism simply does not fall under this topic. Furthermore, if Paul's point was to keep women in their subordinate role, on what basis is the male homogenitality of verse 27 "unnatural"? At that time it was perfectly "natural," it was standard practice in the Roman world, for men to have sex with other men, as long as they observed the pecking order.

Perhaps Paul was being deliberately ambiguous, addressing both a Jewish and a Gentile audience. Perhaps this ambiguity served to suggest to his different listeners a wide range of sexual practices, and Paul's overall point—as argued here—is that in Christ differences in sexual practices are ethically neutral.

The bottom line is that there is no certainty on this matter. Romans 1:26 should not be cited as referring to lesbian sex.

There is a lot at stake in the interpretation of verse 26 for those who want to use the Bible to condemn homosexuality. If this verse does not refer to lesbianism, then nowhere does the Bible even mention it, and condemnation of female homogenitality would have no biblical basis. What sense would the case against homogenitality make if the Bible condemns only male, but not female, homogenital activity?

On the other hand, if the Bible nowhere condemns homogenitality at all—as is the argument here—then the easier reading stands without problem. In verse 26, Paul was not referring to women having sex without men and, echoing Roman culture, condemning it as unnatural. Verse 26 does not refer to female same sex acts but to some kind of heterosexual practices that were considered taboo, unusual or unclean, and perhaps also non-procreative. This interpretation seems the more warranted.

But even if this interpretation is wrong, even if verse 26 is a reference to lesbian sex, the general conclusion argued below must still apply: Romans may refer to same-sex acts, but it intends no ethical condemnation of them.

Social Disapproval, Not Ethical Condemnation

Thus far we have seen that the Greek words translated as "unnatural" would be more accurately translated as "unusual" or "atypical." This realization led to the conclusion that Romans is not portraying male homogenital acts as unethical or morally wrong and that Romans is probably not even referring to lesbian sex.

Now we turn to the two other Greek words that Paul uses in verse 27 to describe the sexual acts he has in mind. He speaks of "degrading" passions and "shameless" acts. Just like the words *para physin*, *atypical*, these words also have no ethical connotation. Both simply refer to social disapproval.

Take "degrading passions," for example. The Greek word translated as "degrading" is *atimia*. It means something "not highly valued," "not held in honor," "not respected." "Ill reputed" or "socially unacceptable" also convey the sense of the word.

That is the very sense in which Paul commonly uses that word. For example, in 2 Corinthians 6:8 and 11:21, Paul applies that word to himself. He notes that he is sometimes held in disrepute or shame because of his commitment to Christ. Evidently, then, to be in *atimia* is not necessarily a bad thing.

Again, in 1 Corinthians 11:14, Paul uses that word to suggest that it is "degrading" for a man to wear long hair. Even though, as we saw above, Paul says this is what "nature" teaches, it is clear that no ethical judgment is intended. Or again, in Romans 9:21, Paul speaks of clay pots fashioned "for dishonor." (This same usage occurs in 2 Timothy 2:20.) That is a polite way of talking about chamber pots, something people do not consider very nice. Finally, in 1 Corinthians 15:43, Paul speaks about our buried bodies as "sown in dishonor [or humiliation], raised in glory."

Those are all the cases in which Paul uses the word *atimia*. In none of them does the Greek word express a moral judgment. So according to his standard usage, when Paul calls certain passions "degrading" in Romans 1:26, he is not saying they are wrong. He is merely saying they do not enjoy social approval.

Basically the same meaning applies to the third word Paul uses to describe same-sex acts: *aschemosyne*, translated as "shameless" in verse 27. Literally the word means "not according to form." You may recognize the English words *scheme* or *schematic* in the middle of that Greek word. The sense of the word is "not nice," "unseemly," "uncomely" or "inappropriate."

In 1 Corinthians 12:23, the prudish Paul uses this word to refer to the "unseemly" or "unpresentable" parts of the body. Of course, he means the genitals. Revelations 16:15 has the exact same usage. Then in 1 Corinthians 13:5, Paul uses this word to describe love: it is not "rude." The King James Version reads, "It doth not behave itself unseemly." Finally, in 1 Corinthians 7, Paul advises people not to marry because he believes that the world is going to end soon. But in verse 36 he says, if this arrangement is embarrassing or disgracing the young woman (because she has no husband), if the man thinks he is "not behaving *properly*" toward her, then they should by all means get married.

Those are all the cases in which Paul uses the word *aschemosyne*. In none of them does the word imply a moral judgment. Rather, they all refer to social regard, to public opinion. Likewise, then, we must presume that in using those words in Romans 1, Paul does not imply that male-male sex is wrong. He merely says it is not looked upon well. It is not considered nice.

Once again the same general conclusion arises. Paul uses certain words to describe male-male sex. A study of these words shows that he makes no ethical condemnation of male-male sex. He merely points out social disapproval of it.

A Convergence of Evidence

Without doubt, Romans does refer to homogenital acts. But equally without doubt, on an historical-critical reading, Romans makes no *ethical* condemnation of those acts. Paul's use of the term *para physin* and his use of *atimia* and *aschemosyne* to describe homogenital acts come together and support the same conclusion. All three words that Paul uses to describe homogenital acts are without ethical weight in his writings.

The Structure of the Passage

Why Bring Up Homogenitality at All?

If Paul does not think that homogenital activity is wrong, why does he say that it is uncomely and disreputable? And why would Paul ever say such things when he is writing to the Romans? Homogenital sex was an everyday part of their world. They thought it perfectly natural for men to be attracted to other men, and they were aware that women were attracted to other women. While there was concern about some excessive and abusive practices and while attitudes about lesbian sex were more negative, the Greeks and Romans saw nothing improper about sex between two men. Why does Paul bring up the topic at all?

Social Disapproval and Jewish Uncleanness

Paul states there is something socially unacceptable about male-male sex. You may recognize here the same sense that we saw in the use of the word *toevah* in Leviticus. Translated "abomination," the meaning is "ritual taboo or impurity," something unacceptable for Jewish society. The word carries with it a sense of disapproval or improperness. Likewise, "dishonorable" passions and "shameless" acts in Romans carry that same sense of "inappropriate," "not socially acceptable."

The parallel with Leviticus seems to be deliberate. There were words, both Hebrew and Greek, that meant "ethically wrong." Those words could have been used in Leviticus 18:22 and 20:13, but, as we have seen, those words were not used. Similarly, Paul also had words that mean "ethically wrong," and he could have used them to refer to male-male sex. But he did not.

In fact, such words of ethical intent occur in that same first chapter of Romans. They occur right before the section on homogenital acts, and they occur right after the section on homogenital acts. But they do not occur within the section on homogenital acts.

In verse 18 Paul notes the "ungodliness and wickedness" of people who suppress the truth. These words translate the Greek *asebeia* and *adikia*. They mean something that is really wrong, unethical behavior, sin. This sense comes through even in the English translation. Then *adikia* occurs again in verse 29. With it there is a long list of things that are clearly wrong in themselves, wicked and evil, not just things that might offend people's sensitivity. Again, even the English makes that perfectly clear. And not one sexual offense occurs in that list.

Right at hand Paul had words that imply ethical condemnation. Paul did not use these words to refer to same-sex acts. His choice of words must have been deliberate.

Just as Leviticus called homogenital acts "unclean" but not sinful nor wrong, so Paul called homogenital acts socially unacceptable but not sinful nor wrong. Both Paul and Leviticus clearly intend to speak of homogenitality only as something inappropriate. The similarity here is real. And, although Leviticus talks of religious disapproval while Romans speaks only of social, the difference is not as big as it seems.

In the ancient Hebrew mind, religious uncleanness and social dishonor went hand in hand. This is clear in the Hebrew Scriptures. According to Genesis 34:14, it is *dishonorable* for Jewish women to be given to uncircumcised men. According to Ezekiel 22:10, a man who has sex with a menstruating woman *shames* her. In Ezekiel 28:10, the phrase "death of the uncircumcised" is a way of saying "a *disgraceful* death." And according to Job 36:14, cult prostitutes are considered to be *the lowest of the low* in society. In all these cases violation of purity laws also entails social disrepute. So the similarity between Leviticus and Romans is real, it is strong and it is deliberate.

Paul Raises a Purity Concern

Therefore, when he talks of homogenitality in Romans, Paul seems to have the Jewish Law in mind. He seems to regard homogenitality as dirty, an uncleanness, an impurity.

Is that the case? Is that why our interpretation of Romans has the same feel as Leviticus? Yes! Obviously so! Paul says as much in verse 24: God gave them up to *impurity* and to *dishonor*. Paul is making an issue over purity.

It must be admitted that Paul's use of the word *impurity* (*akatharsia*) here is out of line with his usage elsewhere (1 Thessalonians 2:3, 4:3-8; 2 Corinthians 12:21; Galatians 5:19; Colossians 3:5-6; Ephesians 4:19, 5:3-5; and perhaps Romans 6:19). Paul had already understood Jesus' teaching that the only real uncleanness is uncleanness of the heart. So for Paul, as for Jesus, impurity generally means moral corruption, and it truly is a matter of ethics. However, in those other places Paul links the word *akatharsia* with things that are clearly wrong and sinful, like greed and covetousness, deceit and trickery, or idolatry. In striking contrast, in Romans 1:24, Paul links uncleanness only with disgrace and shame. As we have seen, these have no ethical connotation for Paul. So Paul's use of *akatharsia* here is peculiar. He is using impurity in the old sense associated with the Jewish Law. But he is not alone in this. When the Jewish Law is in question, other places in the Christian Scriptures also continue to use the word impurity in the Jewish sense (Matthew 23:27; Acts 10:14, 28, 11:8).

But why is Paul making a point of impurity? Jesus and Christianity are not concerned about purity; the Gentile Romans never did have such Jewish concerns. So why does Paul mention it?

The Twofold Effect of Gentile Idolatry

As we have already seen, a close look at the words Paul uses to refer to same-sex acts makes it clear that Paul is not offering an ethical condemnation. He is only pointing out social disapproval. In the terms of ancient Israel, Paul is presenting these acts as "unclean" and "impure."

If we wanted to, we could stop right here. We already have a solid argument: Paul's statement in Romans 1 was not condemning same-sex acts. His vocabulary clearly and consistently supports this conclusion. But a lot more can be said. Other considerations can make this conclusion all the more firm.

We were left with the question, Why would the Christian Paul make an issue of purity? Attention to the structure of this passage of Romans answers this question. Paul wants to teach an important Christian lesson on morality. He wants to emphasize the difference between ritual impurity and real wrong. Following the teaching of Jesus about purity of heart, Paul is drawing a stark distinction between taboo and sin. In order to make this point, Paul breaks his passage into two different sections.

Paul accuses the Gentiles of idolatry: they knew God but did not worship God. And what was the result of their idolatry? Paul says it was twofold. It resulted in uncleanness, and it resulted in real sin.

We have already seen that Paul uses two different kinds of words to describe the Gentiles' deeds. He calls their sexual deeds degrading, shameful, dishonorable. He calls their other deeds wickedness, evil, malice. The words themselves show a deliberate contrast between what is socially objectionable and what is ethically wrong. Paul has two categories of deeds in mind.

The structure of Paul's argument highlights that contrast in vocabulary. Three times Paul repeats the phrase, "God gave them up." This repetition divides his statement into different sections. Paul is arguing that, because they did not worship God, two situations resulted.

Paul begins verse 24 with "Therefore *God gave them up* in the lusts of their hearts to impurity, to the *degrading* of their bodies." This statement introduces the first effect, impurity. But, as Paul often does (Galatians 1:5; Romans 9:5, 11:33-36; Philippians 4:20), here too he digresses in the praise of God, the Creator, "who is blessed forever! Amen" (verse 25). He catches himself and gets back on track in verse 26. We can see that he is getting back to his original line of argument because he repeats the catch phrase that structures his argument and he repeats his key word: "For this reason *God gave them up* to *degrading* passions." Then Paul talks of the first effect of Gentile idolatry: uncleanness in sexual matters. So, although the phrase, "God gave them up," occurs three times, the phrase actually divides the passage into only two sections. Because of his digression, Paul has to say "God gave them up" twice to make his first point.

Then, in verse 28 Paul moves on to the second effect. He recalls his main argument: neglect of God brought these things on the Gentiles. He begins verse 28 with "And." Evidently, he is introducing something new. This time he goes on to talk of evil, malice and real sins. He writes, "And since they did not see fit to acknowledge God, God gave them up to a base mind and things that should not be done." Thus, Paul introduces a second section of this passage.

Still another consideration indicates that Paul divided his statement into two sections. Verses 24-27 speak of sexual matters, but the long list of evils that follows in verses 28-32 does not include a single sexual matter. The contrast is striking, and it must be deliberate.

Of course, the King James Version includes "adultery" in verse 28, but this inclusion is now commonly known to be a mistake. It resulted because the King James Version, though generally quite an accurate translation, relied on Greek manuscripts that had been corrupted over the centuries. The King James Version is an accurate translation of defective texts. The word *adultery* does not occur at this point in the more reliable manuscripts. We could even understand how the word *adultery* perhaps crept into those manuscripts. It occurs right next to the word *evil*. And the Greek words are very similar: adultery is *porneia*, and evil is *poneria*. A scribe could easily have made a copying error.

Finally, there is a telling grammatical consideration that suggests that this passage falls into two sections. When in verse 29 Paul says "They were filled with every kind of wickedness," the original Greek uses the perfect participle *pepleromenous*. Translated more literally this passage would read, "God gave them up, namely, them who were *already filled* with every kind of wickedness." In Greek, this use of a perfect participle indicates that the time of their "being filled" occurred before the time of God's "giving them up." They were already filled with wickedness and then God surrendered them to it—and to impurity, as well. The point is that the impurity should not be run together with the wickedness, for the time of the wickedness and the time of the impurity are not the same. The wickedness was part of the picture before the impurities. In standard translations, *pepleromenous* has been taken to indicate intensity: "so totally filled were they...." But "already filled" is an accurate translation.

Hence, the conclusion: writing to the Romans, Paul has two different things in mind, uncleanness and real wrong. Both the structure of Paul's passage and the content of Paul's argument show that this is the case. According to Paul, not only did their idolatry lead the Gentiles into other ethical wrongs, wickedness, real sins, which do merit death, but because of their idolatry, God finally also "gave them up" to impurities, naughty conduct, shameful and disreputable things—like homogenital acts.

Bernadette Brooten denies Romans 1:24-32 falls into two sections, one about sexual practices that are socially disapproved and a second about wrong behaviors that are real sins. Rather than see two sections in this passage, she argues that a spiral logic is at stake. Supposedly, Paul circles round and round the same one topic, going deeper and deeper, and in the process links the sexual matters in verses 26 and 27 with the sins in verses 28 to 32. Then the sexual practices appear to be one with that long list of sins and even, as verse 32 says, merit death.

The "spiral interpretation" of this passage is not convincing. Too many facets of the passage point to its two-part structure—the specific announcement of two different topics, differences in vocabulary, differences in content, a repeated introductory phrase, use of the word "And," the tense of the linking participle. The further analysis that follows will also show that a two-part structure makes perfect sense in the overall argument of Paul's Letter to the Romans, whereas the spiral interpretation does not. To run together the section on sexual impurities with the section on real wrongs must be one of the commonest and most serious mistakes in interpreting Romans 1. As it is, Paul was really writing about two different things. Impurity, convention, custom or taboo is one thing; real wrong, evil or sin is something very different.

The Overall Plan of the Letter to the Romans

Disapproval of Male-Male Sex?

Well, that is a partial answer to the question, Why would the Christian Paul make an issue of purity? He wants to teach a lesson on morality, namely, violations of social expectations and impurities according to the Jewish Law are not the same thing as sin. So, in opening his letter to the Romans, Paul talks about impurity as one result of Gentile idolatry, and he mentions homogenitality as an example of such impurity.

But this still sounds pretty bad. Impurity may not be sin, yet according to Paul, impurity results from idolatry. Then, same-sex acts are supposedly the result of Gentile idolatry! Paul does not seem to cast them in a very positive light.

Does Paul disapprove of homogenitality, even though he says it is just an impurity and not real sin? It certainly seems that way—at least for the time being.

But here's what's going on. At this point Paul appears to be sympathizing with the common Jewish feeling that the Gentiles are dirty. But this appearance is only a ploy. Paul will use this Jewish prejudice to teach his lesson about Christian community.

In the first chapter of Romans, Paul put himself in the middle of a petty name-calling bout. He seems to be playing a game of we're-better-than-you. Paul is quoting Jewish prejudice! And he seems to be supporting it. Ah, but he quotes it precisely to counter and reject it. Paul will use that nasty rivalry between the Jews and the Gentiles to his own advantage.

Paul is playing on Jewish self-righteousness. He is echoing the Jewish claim to moral superiority. Paul begins his letter by allowing that both sin and uncleanness are the twofold result of Gentile idolatry. And the Jews in Rome would certainly applaud him—and he would have them eating out of his hand!

"The Due Penalty for their Error"

That understanding also explains another aspect of the Romans passage, and being able to explain this aspect strengthens the overall argument.

Verse 27 says that because men commit shameful acts with men they receive "in their own persons the due penalty for their error." There has been much debate about what this verse means. A very common understanding of this verse sees homosexuality as the error, and sexually transmitted diseases or even AIDS is supposedly the due penalty.

But that interpretation doesn't make sense. Heterosexuals also have sexually transmitted diseases, and if AIDS is God's punishment for homosexuality, God must love lesbians, for of all social groups they are least at risk for AIDS. Obviously, this text needs a better interpretation.

Besides, what is translated as "in their own persons" reads differently in the Greek. A better translation would be "among themselves." The reference is not to individuals and their persons but to the Gentiles as a whole, to their culture.

Moreover, the word "penalty" offers a loaded translation; it carries a negative connotation that is not in the Greek. The Greek word simply means "recompense," "deserts" or "payment," which could be positive, negative or neutral.

Given what we already understand about the first chapter of Romans, a very easy explanation of verse 27 arises. The error Paul refers to is not homosexuality but Gentile idolatry. Idolatry is his concern throughout the whole of that chapter: they knew God but did not worship God. And the recompense that comes to the Gentiles for not worshipping God is the uncleanness that is a regular part of their culture.

Paul is saying that, in addition to committing real sin, the Gentiles are also soiled. Their culture is filled with unclean practices. Both sin and impurities abound among the Gentiles. And, of course, Paul is speaking from the perspective of the self-righteous Jews.

Paul's reasoning differs from what *we* generally think. We would say that, because people sin, they are idolaters, they distance themselves from God. But Paul's Jewish heritage leads him to see this matter in reverse. Because people abandon God, wickedness abounds among them. For Paul the root of all evil is disregard for God. This idolatry, this turning from God, is the gravest of all human faults. For Paul and the Jewish religion, this is sin—and all the things we would call *sins* are merely expressions of this core fault.

So wrongdoings and impurity are the result of Gentile idolatry, the result of their not worshipping God as the Jews do. Not acknowledging the Jewish God, they do not acknowledge the Jewish Law, so they do not share the Jewish purity rules. Therefore, they are unclean. The dirtiness of the Gentiles comes from their idolatry.

There it is, plain and simple. Rid the text of the prejudices that the 21st Century reads into it and all the pieces fall together. The text makes perfect sense. The only requirement is to recognize Paul's argument that Gentile idolatry has two very different results: uncleanness and sin. Paul raises the issue of homogenitality only as an uncleanness. It is the recompense of Gentile idolatry.

The Self-righteousness of the Jewish Christians

All this talk of uncleanness may be foreign to us, but it was at the center of the emergence of Christianity as a religion different from Judaism. Keeping or not keeping the Jewish Law was a hot issue in early Christianity. The "Council of Jerusalem," recorded in Acts 15, decreed that Gentiles converted to Christianity need not be circumcised nor keep the rest of the Jewish Law. But arguments and rivalries still went on. The issue was still quite alive.

For example, Paul wrote to the church at Corinth rebuking them for disputes during their common meals. Evidently, arguments over clean and unclean food were disrupting the Lord's Supper (1 Corinthians 11:17-22). In another instance, Paul confronted Peter and "opposed him to his face" because Peter refused to eat with the Gentile Christians. Jewish Christians were putting strong pressure on Peter to keep the purity requirements of the Law (Galatians 2:11-14).

Many Jewish Christians still kept the Jewish Law, and they felt some sense of superiority because of that. Paul, of course, took the side of the Gentiles, teaching that faith in Christ and not fidelity to the Law is what justifies a person (Galatians 2:16). Paul was well known for his position.

Paul's Appeal to the Jewish Christians

So when Paul wrote to the Romans, he had quite a feat to accomplish. He intended to visit Rome, and he wanted the Christian church there to welcome him. But the Christians in Rome were like the Christians almost everywhere else: a mix of both Jewish and Gentile converts. Paul had to appeal to both sides without offending either of them, and they were often at each other's throats.

How did Paul handle the matter? Pretty shrewdly. He started his letter by addressing the Jewish Christians, and he played on their sense of superiority. Paul wanted to win the good will of the Jewish Christians. At first he would appear to take their side. He said what they felt, what they might even boast, that the Gentiles are a dirty lot. He put the Gentiles down by pointing out their homogenital practices.

Ah, so that is where the question of homogenital impurity comes in!

But already by chapter two, Paul turns the tables on the Jewish Christians and rejects their prejudices. He approaches the matter cautiously. At first he addresses them anonymously: "Therefore you have no excuse, O human being, whoever you are, when you judge another" (Romans 2:1). But by verse 17 it is clear that Paul is addressing no one other than the Jewish Christians: "But if you call yourself a Jew and rely on the law..."

So the Jewish Christians have their circumcision, and they avoid impurities. But, as Paul points out, their real sins still break the Law. They steal, commit adultery and rob temples. Therefore, the Jewish Christians have no right to boast about the Jewish Law. They have no right to look down on the Gentile Christians.

Paul hooks the Jewish Christians on their sense of superiority over the Gentile impurities, and then he reels them in. He undermines any sense of superiority the Jewish Christians might have. He disqualifies their self-righteousness over not engaging in dirty behaviors. Incisively he makes his point. In the face of faith in Christ and Christ's call for purity of heart, ritual behaviors and impurities do not matter. "A person is a Jew who is one inwardly, and real circumcision is a matter of the heart— it is spiritual and not literal" (Romans 2:29).

Paul's Appeal to the Gentile Christians

But Paul doesn't let the Gentile Christians off the hook, either. In Paul's mind and God's plan, the Gentiles come second. But Paul does eventually address them.

In chapter 9, Paul begins to turn attention to them, gently drawing them into the discussion. As he did with the Jews in Romans 2:1, at first he refers to the Gentiles only indirectly, in the third person, as "they" and as "the Gentiles." But by 11:13 Paul puts it to the Gentiles, addressing them directly: "Now I am speaking to you Gentiles." He rebukes them for thinking themselves better than the Jewish Christians, the first to be God's chosen people.

Homogenitality in the Overall Plan of Paul's Letter

We have seen that Paul's terminology in Romans 1 presents male homogenital acts as socially unacceptable or impure—but not as ethically wrong. Then we saw that the very structure of that passage highlights the difference between taboo or impurity, on the one hand, and real wrong, injustice, or sin, on the other. Now, aware that Paul is writing to a Christian community split between Jewish and Gentile converts, we can understand how Paul's mention of homogenitality fits into the whole Letter to the Romans.

Paul structures his Letter to the Romans so that he can win the favor of both the Jewish and the Gentile Christians. He tries to appeal to both while keeping them in harmony with one another. He wants all to know the salvation that comes to everyone who has faith, "to the Jew first and also to the Greek" (Romans 1:16). That is his gospel: grace and peace to all from God and the Lord Jesus Christ (Romans 1:7). "For as in one body we have many members, and not all the members have the same function, so we, who are many, are one body in Christ, and individually we are members one of another" (Romans 12:4-5).

Paul's prayer is that the Christians at Rome "live in harmony with one another, according to Christ Jesus" (Romans 15:5). Paul does not want false issues to divide them, so he insists, "I know and am persuaded in the Lord Jesus that nothing is unclean in itself" (Romans 14:14).

This bold statement, nothing is unclean, is a high point of the Letter to the Romans. At this point in chapter 14, Paul is talking about clean and unclean foods. But he does not simply say "no foods are unclean." Rather, he makes a sweeping statement: *nothing* is unclean. In chapter 1, he raised the question about the supposed uncleanness of homogenital acts. Now his statement in chapter 14 confirms what he argued throughout his letter. Customs about food, the practice of circumcision, differences in sexual behavior—no purity requirements or cultural variations have ethical importance in themselves.

Now Paul's reference to same-sex acts finally makes complete sense. Seen in the context of the whole Letter to the Romans, that reference serves a rhetorical function. It is part of Paul's plan to win the good will of his Jewish Christian readers. Then he uses the same issue to make his point: the ritual requirements of the Jewish Law are irrelevant in Christ.

Why did he choose homogenitality and not some other purity issue? Why not talk about unclean foods or about circumcision? Well, from the current century's point of view, the answer may sound crazy. But from a first-century point of view, it makes perfect sense: in those days homogenital activity was a safe topic.

Paul could not open his letter with talk about clean and unclean foods. Debate over foods was still splitting the Christian communities. Likewise, circumcision was too sensitive an issue. But evidently homogenitality was not. It was an obvious point of difference, and apparently there was no intense argument over it.

The Jews were well aware that Leviticus forbade male-male sex only as an impurity; they would not say the Gentiles were sinning because of their homogenital practices. Remember how casually later rabbis treated the case of male Gentile converts "sporting with boys." Paul's mention of homogenitality could let the Jewish Christians feel superior without, in anyone's eyes, accusing the Gentile Christians of real sin.

At the same time, the whole Gentile world was well aware of the Jews' peculiar attitude toward homogenital acts. The Gentiles just chuckled and shrugged the whole thing off. They would not be offended if Paul raised that issue in his letter. Besides, they knew that Paul was the "apostle to the Gentiles" (Romans 11:13). Surely, if anything, he was on their side.

So unlike other purity issues, homogenitality was the one that would work. With it, Paul could do what he needed to do in writing to the Romans:

- first gain the sympathy of the Jewish Christians by seeming to side with their prejudices;
- next show that the Jewish Christians were as guilty as anyone else in breaking the Jewish Law;
- then argue that in Christ the Jewish Law was superseded and that, above all, purity issues in the Law do not matter;
- and thus incline the Jewish Christians to better acceptance of the Gentile Christians;
- and finally rebuke the Gentile Christians sharply for any smugness they might by then be feeling.

The mention of homogenitality, Gentile "dirtiness," becomes a clever rhetorical ploy in Paul's presentation of "the gospel of God" (Romans 1:1).

Another Confirmation of the Same Conclusion

In Romans, homogenitality serves merely as an instance of Gentile "uncleanness," judged by Jewish standards. Paul introduces this "uncleanness" precisely to make the point that such matters have no importance in Christ. This is clear from every consideration already presented. Moreover, only if that is really the case does the whole structure of Romans make sense.

This interpretation completely explains the reference to male-male sex in Romans. First, attention to the vocabulary in the passage, second, study of the structure of the passage and third, analysis of the overall plan of the letter—all lead to the same conclusion. The Letter to the Romans certainly does not consider homogenital acts to be sinful. Indeed, the success of Paul's Letter to the Romans depends on this being so.

A further conclusion follows. Not only did Paul not think homogenital acts are sinful. More than that, he seems to have been deliberately unconcerned about them. In his considered treatment of the matter, he teaches that in itself homogenital activity is ethically neutral.

The Sin that Paul Would Condemn

Once again, a sad irony surrounds this matter. There is a religious lesson to be learned.

A long-standing and naive reading of the Scriptures has led many sincere followers of Jesus astray. They oppose and oppress lesbian and gay people in the name of the apostle Paul. Bolstered by societal prejudice and zealous in their sexual self-righteousness, Christians have been misreading Saint Paul's Letter to the Romans and rejecting members of the Christian community because of it.

Yet to insure the unity of believers was a major reason for Paul's writing. Paul insisted on faith and love as the things that really matter in Christ. But by misunderstanding Paul's argument, people unwittingly rely on tastes and customs instead of the word of God. They argue about what's dirty or clean, dispute who's pure and impure, and pit heterosexual against homosexual. Thus, they divide and splinter the church over what does not matter in Christ. In God's name they foment hatred and fuel oppression and disrupt society at large. They commit a grave injustice, the very offense that Paul's letter meant to counter.

This is a sad state of affairs. It is unworthy of followers of Jesus.

104

Seven. 1 Corinthians & 1 Timothy: Abusive Male-Male Sex

Two other texts in the Christian Testament have something to do with homogenital acts, and they can be treated together. Their meaning depends on the translation of two Greek words—*malakoi* and *arsenokoitai*—and their translation is highly debated.

The bottom line on this discussion is as follows: *Malakoi* has no specific reference to homogenitality. On the other hand, *arsenokoitai*, which occurs in two texts, *may be* some kind of reference to male same-sex acts. If it is, these texts condemn wanton, lewd, irresponsible male homogenital acts but not homogenital acts in general.

Wide Variation in Translations

In both texts those words occur in lists of sinners of various kinds. It is hard to determine what any words in a list mean because the words have no context to help suggest a meaning. All that can be determined in the present case is that the words refer to something evil. But to what?

In 1 Corinthians 6:9-10, the 1952 Revised Standard Version translates the two words as one. The result is as follows:

> Do not be deceived: neither the immoral, nor idolaters, nor adulterers, nor homosexuals (*oute malakoi oute arsenokoitai*), nor thieves, nor the greedy, nor drunkards, nor revilers, nor robbers will inherit the kingdom of God.

The 1977 version of that Bible translates those two words as "sexual perverts." The 1989 New Revised Standard Version translates the two words separately as "male prostitutes and sodomites."

1 Timothy 1:9-10 in that same 1989 translation reads as follows:

> the law is laid down not for the innocent but for the lawless and disobedient, for the godless and sinners, for the unholy and profane, for those who kill their father or mother, for murderers, fornicators, sodomites (*arsenokoitai*), slave traders, liars, perjurers and whatever else is contrary to the sound teaching...

Various modern versions translate those words differently. *Arsenokoitai* is rendered as "homosexuals," "sodomites," "child molesters," "perverts," "homosexual perverts," sexual perverts" or "people of infamous habits."

Malakoi is rendered as "catamites," "the effeminate," "boy prostitutes" or even as "sissies." The 1985 New Jerusalem Bible provides the most accurate translation: "the self-indulgent." But until the Reformation in the 16th Century and in Roman Catholicism until the 20th Century, the word *malakoi* was thought to mean "masturbators." It seems that as prejudices changed, so have translations of the Bible.

The Catholic Church's recent *New American Bible* invites the same cynicism. It translated *arsenokoitai* as "practicing homosexuals." How amazing! A first-century text would now seem to teach exactly what Roman Catholicism began teaching only in the mid-1970s: to be homosexual is no fault, but to engage in homogenital acts is wrong. The attempt to nuance the translation is certainly understandable and welcome. Still, this translation reads a whole new worldview into the original Greek text, for there was no elaborated awareness of sexual orientation in first-century Christianity. Even worse, "practicing homosexuals"—like "homosexuals" and "homosexual perverts" in those other translations—includes

106

women as well as men. But as we shall see, *arsenokoitai* certainly refers only to men. At the instigation of Dignity/USA, a support group for lesbian and gay Catholics and their friends, the editors of the New American Bible agreed to delete the term *practicing homosexuals*. In its place they substituted *sodomites*, which is hardly much better.

The Preferred Conclusion

The variety of translations shows that this whole discussion is very tenuous. The interpretations presented below are all that scholarship can offer: "the best available opinion of the day." There is no real certainty about what these texts mean.

Given that fact, the conclusion should be very simple. Nobody knows for certain what these words mean, so to use them to condemn homosexuals is really dishonest and unfair.

In light of the interpretation given to Romans above, that conclusion does seem warranted. If our longest biblical treatment of same-sex acts shows Paul indifferent to the matter, the benefit of the doubt about *arsenokoitai* should fall in the same direction. If in Romans, Paul does not condemn homogenitality, it must be wrong to use 1 Corinthians 6:9 and 1 Timothy 1:10 to condemn it. These two texts depend on one obscure Greek word. Such uncertainty hardly provides a just basis for accusing people of sinning before God.

Still, the evidence really is not conclusive. What if *arsenokoitai* does refer to male same-sex acts? To be fair to all sides, it would be good to consider the implications. Then no one could object that this book is just "interpreting away" one Bible text after another. But all the same, the main point of this book will only be confirmed once again. This analysis will show that the Bible nowhere offers a blanket condemnation of same-sex acts. That is, even allowing the more damning interpretation in the case of *arsenokoitai*, the biblical teaching comes out quite nuanced. Abuse and exploitation are forbidden, but not homogenitality in itself. A study of those two Greek words will support this conclusion.

Malakoi: The Self-Indulgent

First, consider the term *malakos* (the plural is *malakoi*). It is a very common word. Literally it means "soft." It is said of clothing in Matthew 11:8; it could be used to describe warm butter. In the ancient world, it was sometimes used to belittle men–and put down women in the process. Then the word was taken to mean something like "effeminate," "women-like." Applied to moral matters, as John Boswell suggests, it could mean "loose," "wanton," "unrestrained" or "undisciplined." This seems the most sensible translation for *malakoi* in 1 Corinthians 6:9.

In contrast, L. William Countryman thinks that the lists of sins in 1 Corinthians 6:9 and 1 Timothy 1:10 parallel the list of the Ten Commandments. So he looks in *malakoi* and *arsenokoitai* for something related to both sex and money, linking the commandment about adultery with the next commandment about stealing. Thus, he holds to the older thought that *malakoi* means "masturbators"—but he would add an overtone of financial wastefulness. In that case, the colloquial English term, "jerkoff," would catch the sense of the Greek. It would refer to a person so devoted to personal pleasure (masturbation?!) as to lack financial responsibility and good sense. This interpretation seems strained.

Yet another scholar, Robin Scroggs, has tried to link the term *malakos* with a particular expression of homogenitality in the ancient world. He calls this type "the effeminate call boy." These would be free (not slave) youths who chose to offer themselves for male-male sex in exchange for money—and for the thrill of it. Mark Antony, famous for his later romance with Cleopatra, had indulged in such prostitution as a youth. As these men grew older and tried to preserve their youthful looks, they might style and perfume their hair, rouge their face, and remove facial and body hair. "Effeminate" was, indeed, an insult thrown their way.

To be sure, *malakos* could be translated "effeminate," but there is very little evidence—and it is forced—that the term *malakos* was specifically linked with this effeminate *homosexual* style. Effeminacy was simply not associated with male-male sex in the ancient world, though a man who allowed himself to be penetrated might be called "effeminate." But on the other hand, *malakos* was also applied to men who primped themselves in order to attract women or who were lazy, wanton or loose. Besides, as a contrast with "virile" or "manly" in certain texts, "undisciplined" or "weak" would translate *malakos* as well as "effeminate."

So the conclusion is that malakos simply does not refer to same-sex activity. 1 Corinthians 6:9 uses *malakos* to make a general condemnation of moral looseness and undisciplined (and perhaps also lewd, lustful and lascivious) behavior. The New Jerusalem Bible presents this accurate meaning by translating *malakos* as "the self-indulgent."

Various Interpretations of *Arsenokoitai*

Next, consider the term *arsenokoitai*. It is even more difficult to explain. 1 Corinthians is our earliest record of the word. It occurs in the Bible only there and in 1 Timothy. In other literature it occurs in only a half dozen places and then almost always in vice lists. So scholars are left guessing what it might mean.

The word is a compound of two parts, and they are easy enough to translate. *Arseno-* refers to men, male humans, plain and simple. *Koitai* comes from the word that means bedroom or bed and refers to "lying" with—that is, having sex with—someone. More precisely, it refers to the active partner in sexual intercourse, the one who penetrates.

So the literal English translation of *arsenokoitai* would be "manlier," "man-sleeper" or, more graphically, "man-penetrator."

But when the two parts of the word are put together, it is not clear what the word means. Is "man" to emphasize the gender of the sexual agent: male? Or is "man" to indicate the object of the sexual act? That is, does *arsenokoitai* mean a man who has sex with others, or does it mean a man who has sex with men? In the first case the word would refer to a man who is the active partner in intercourse with anyone, female or male. In the second case the word would refer quite specifically to a man who is the active partner in a male-male anal sex. But from the word itself there is no way of telling which of these two meanings—or what other meaning—might have been intended. Language is not always logical. In English the word "lady killer" means neither a lady who kills nor a person who kills ladies but a man who knows how to charm women.

Scholars differ on their interpretations. Boswell suggests that *arsenokoitai* refers to male prostitutes. They were available to have sex with either women or men.

Countryman also believes that *arsenokoitai* may refer to male prostitutes but specifically to prostitutes who cultivate the elderly so they might inherit their estates. The Roman poet Juvenal makes sport of one such heterosexual affair.

If *arsenokoitai* does refer to male prostitutes, the objection is not to having sex, whether with a person of the opposite or the same sex. The objection is to some specific form of male prostitution. The little evidence we have does suggest that *arsenokoitai* has something to do with sexual foul play around money.

Scroggs proposes an interpretation that could also have something to do with prostitution but prostitution of a particular form and strictly between men. He takes *arsenokoitai* to refer to the active partner in male-male sex, but he believes that such sex always occurred between an older man and a young boy. So in his interpretation the sin is not male-male sex *per se* but child abuse, pederasty. As already noted, Scroggs takes *malakoi* to refer to the passive pederast partner, the supposed soft and effeminate call boy. So, according to Scroggs, these two words constitute a pair, and the call boy and the child-abusing man are both condemned.

Without Scroggs' emphasis on male prostitution and pederasty, other scholars also commonly take *malakoi* and *arsenokoitai* to be a pair. This supposed pair of Greek words is said to condemn homogenital activity in general. This particular interpretation is found in the current, standard New Testament Greek dictionaries, which do not yet reflect the latest scholarship, but do reflect the sexual biases of the mid- to late-20th Century. Similarly, this interpretation was behind the translation in the revised (and now, on this point, re-revised) New American Bible: "boy prostitutes and sodomites." And this interpretation is behind the translation in the 1987 New Revised Standard Version: "male prostitutes and sodomites."

As already argued, there is simply no specific reference to homogenital activity in the term *malakoi,* so pairing it with *arsenokoitai* is wrong. However, it is possible that *arsenokoitai* does refer to some form of male homogenital behavior. Some scholars think they have found a clue to a possible explanation of this obscure two-part Greek word. That clue is not in the Greek usage but, rather, in the Hebrew usage. They suggest that *arsenokoitai* might be a literal translation of a Hebrew term.

Man-Lying-with-Man Revisited

Though the Greeks had many terms for the various aspects of male homogenital behavior, Hebrew had no word for it at all. Recall that Leviticus had to use the clumsy phrase, "the man who lies with a male the lyings of a women." Note how the familiar word stems, *arsen-* and *koit-*, appear in the Septuagint Greek translation of this phrase: *hos an koimethe meta arsenos koiten gunaikos.* Moreover, in a shorthand form of this phrase, as a way of speaking of male same-sex acts, the rabbis supposedly began to use the Hebrew words *mishkav zakur* (lying of a male) or *mishkav bzakur* (lying with a male). Translated literally for the Greek-speaking Jews, the result could well be *arseno-koitai,* "man liers," "those who lie with a male."

In summary, the suggestion is this: the Greek-speaking Jews coined the term *arsenokoitai.* They created the term by translating literally the rabbis' shorthand Hebrew phrase into Greek. If this is the case, and there is no certainty about it, *arsenokoitai* relates to the prohibition of male same-sex acts in Leviticus 18:22 and 20:13, and it means men who have penetrative sex with men. A study of the few non-biblical places where this word occurs and a study of the earliest translations of the Christian Testament into Latin, Syriac and Coptic could lend some support to this interpretation, but in this matter nothing is conclusive.

So, it seems, 1 Corinthians 6:9 and 1 Timothy 1:10 may be repeating the prohibition in Leviticus 18:22.

Questions about *Arsenokoitai* in the Christian Testament

Then how very peculiar! Leviticus forbids male-male sex as an impurity according to the Jewish Law. But Jesus and Christian teaching rejected purity concerns as a basis for morality.

In fact, as we have seen, Paul's Letter to the Romans makes that very point, using male-male sex itself as an example. But Paul also wrote 1 Corinthians; and 1 Timothy, though not written by Paul himself, follows the Pauline tradition. Then why would these letters condemn what Romans shrugs off?

Of course, throughout the Roman Empire, Corinth was notorious for its sexual depravity. Perhaps Paul's concern about Corinth was different from his concern about Rome. Or perhaps Paul had revised his thinking between writing to the Corinthians and to the Romans. But if so, what about 1 Timothy, written much later than Romans? As often happens when disciples take up the teaching of their charismatic master, had the later "Pauline tradition" become more strict than Paul himself? That is what happened with Paul's teachings about slavery and the behavior expected of women, as we have seen.

Those questions leave much to ponder, and we may never have the complete answers to them. The historical evidence is scanty. But if we can understand more precisely what *arsenokoitai* was referring to, we may at least be able to make some sense of the matter.

Using Lists of Sins

Recall that in both 1 Corinthians and 1 Timothy *arsenokoitai* occurs in a list of various sinners. Scholars are pretty well agreed that those lists are not Paul's own.

Note, for example, that in 1 Corinthians the list names sinners who are excluded from the kingdom of God. Although in passing Paul does mention the kingdom of God in Romans 14:17, 1 Corinthians 4:20, 15:24, and 15:50, and in Galatians 5:21, the kingdom of God is simply not a developed theme in Pauline teaching. Besides, it is clear that Paul is not specifically concerned about any of the particular sins in the list. He does not go back to write at length about, or even mention, any of them.

Thus, it appears that Paul just borrowed stock lists of supposed vices from the culture at large. He is encouraging his readers to be good people, and he does that by reminding them of the evils of the day. He just repeats the list of wrongs that people generally decried in his society, rhetorically piling up a heap of vices to overwhelm his readers, as was the style of the day. A current example would be someone today talking about "drugs, guns, teenage violence, child abuse and the breakdown of the family."

The point is that this list of sins is not Paul's own. It comes from some other source and reflects society at large. Then, to understand what was being condemned as *arsenokoitai*, we need to know what first-century critics condemned as male-male sex.

The Decadence of the First Century

When the Greeks wrote about male-male love, they extolled it as the highest form of affection. It included emotional attachment and deep concern, friendship and shared values, and commitment to a common task. Sex was not the main focus of the relationship. Virtue was. Even when the relationship involved an adult and a youth, as it often did, the older man was a mentor to the younger one. He introduced the youth to culture and learning, and encouraged honorable behavior.

In the first-century Roman Empire, however, moral decadence was rampant. Social critics of the day decried the low life. Men sought out boys and other men for sex—the critics complained and supposed—as a novelty in the face of overly abundant female prostitution. There was too much sex all around—the critics lamented—and same-sex practices were the obvious sign of that. Men kept and abused slaves as objects of their lust. Attractive girls and boys were kidnapped and sold into sexual slavery. (This may be why "kidnappers" occurs next to *arsenokoitai* in the list of sins in 1 Timothy 1:10.) As was already noted, Robin Scroggs even argues that the whole "model of homosexuality" of the day was pederastic. That is, it always involved an older man and a young boy or youth. Scroggs' position seems too simple. Still, this much is clear: social critics of the day thought of exploitation, inequality, abuse and lust when they thought of male-male sex.

Therefore, that is what the first-century moralists were condemning when they objected to same-sex behavior: exploitation, inequality, abuse and lust. That is what the Greek-speaking Jews were likewise condemning in Roman society. Then, supposing that *arsenokoitai* does refer to male-male sex, we must conclude that the term condemns some kind of abusive sex.

Translating and Interpreting *arsenokoitai*

When 1 Corinthians 6:9 and 1 Timothy 1:10 are understood in their cultural context, the problem of translating *arsenokoitai* into English is apparent. This one word bottles up a whole worldview, and it is not the worldview of our day. No simple translation, but only a broad explanation, can adequately express its meaning.

Assuming for the sake of discussion that *arsenokoitai* does refer to male-male sex, to say that those texts condemn "homosexuals" or "homosexuality" is incorrect. The problem is not just that one could be homosexual without engaging in homogenital acts. And the problem is not just that "homosexual" includes women while *arsenokoitai* certainly does not. The problem is bigger than that. To say "homosexual" implies a psychological and sociological understanding of sexual orientation that was foreign to the early Christian world.

Even to say that *arsenokoitai* refers to "sex-between-men" is not accurate. For in using this term, the first-century authors had particular abuses in mind, and not all sex between men includes these abuses.

The contemporary gay subculture has derogatory terms that apply to some of the abuses suggested by these biblical texts. "Chicken hawk" refers to men who take advantage of attractive, inexperienced, young gay men. "Slut" and "whore" are insulting names that refer to men who are wildly promiscuous and unrestrained in their sexual desire, men who will have sex with anyone they can "make." But these contemporary terms, though validly suggestive, are hardly appropriate biblical translations for the first-century *arsenokoitai*. These terms, too, are closely tied to their own cultural context.

Neither does the Bible's own circumlocution *men lying with men* provide a satisfactory translation of *arsenokoitai*. For the meaning of these words changed within the Bible itself, and the meaning has again changed in our day. Initially, Leviticus condemns "men lying with men," but an understanding of that whole text and its culture make clear that its condemnation applies to something irrelevant both to early Christianity and to most of our contemporary Western world. That something is ritual impurity, violation of the ancient Jewish taboos that surrounded a man's Jewish identity. Later, using the Greek term *arsenokoitai*, two texts in the Christian Testament perhaps reiterate the Hebrew condemnation of men lying with men. But an understanding of these texts shows that these very same words apply to something very different again. That something would be the abuse, exploitation and lust associated with male-male sex in the first-century Roman Empire. But at the turn of the 21st Century, that is hardly what the English words *men lying with men* mean. Today this phrase

114

suggests male homosexuality—which, according to contemporary scientific understanding, implies a normal variation in sexual attraction that inclines men to emotional and genital intimacy with each other.

It may not be altogether possible to translate in one or two English words what *arsenokoitai* really means. So, caught in a distorting time warp, the Christian Testament may ever continue to support homophobic and unchristian attitudes and behavior. Maybe some passages of the Bible just ought to be deleted—or at least never read in public! Nonetheless, it is possible to state simply and with certainty what 1 Corinthians 6:9 and 1 Timothy 1:10 do *not* mean. Whether we take *arsenokoitai* to refer to male-male sex or not, the conclusion is the same. These texts intend no blanket condemnation of homosexuality, nor even of homogenitality.

The Lesson of 1 Corinthians 6:9 and 1 Timothy 1:10

What is the positive teaching of 1 Corinthians 6:9 and 1 Timothy 1:10 regarding male-male sex today? Biblical opposition to prostitution, incest or adultery does not forbid male-female sex acts as such. What the Bible opposes throughout is *abuse* of heterosexuality. Likewise, if *arsenokoitai* does refer to male-male sex, these texts do not forbid male homogenitality as such. In first-century, Greek-speaking, Jewish Christianity, *arsenokoitai* would have referred to exploitative, lewd and wanton sex between men. This, and not male-male sex in general, is what the term would imply. This, then, and not male-male sex in general, is what these biblical texts oppose.

Across the board in sexual matters, the Bible calls for mutual respect, caring and responsible sharing—in a loaded word, love. The violation of these, but not sex in general, is what the Bible condemns. The lesson in 1 Corinthians 6:9 and 1 Timothy 1:10 is that this principle applies equally to hetero- and homosexuality.

Eight. Other Supposed References to Homosexuality

There are a number of other texts in the Bible that are sometimes said to refer to homosexuality, and there is an argument against homosexuality based on the Bible's positive teaching about sex. None of these is really part of biblical teaching on homosexuality. But to make clear why this is the case, this chapter will briefly consider these matters. Finally, this chapter will also consider some instances of homosexual relationships in the Bible, including one that Jesus encountered.

The "Alien Flesh" in Jude

The most debated of those texts that allegedly refer to homosexuality is verse 7 in the short, one-chapter letter of Jude. Except for a few who continue to insist that the sin of Sodom was male-male sex, Scripture scholars today simply do not see homogenitality in this text. Nonetheless, like any vague text in the Bible, people can take it to mean what they want, and some modern translations encourage misinterpretation.

Jude faults the people of Sodom for lusting after "strange" or "alien" flesh. That is clearly what the Greek says—*sarkos heteras*. The King James translation of the Bible accurately presents this meaning:

"Even as Sodom and Gomorrah and the cities about them in like manner, giving themselves over to fornication, and going after strange flesh, are set forth as an example, suffering the vengeance of eternal fire" (Jude 7).

What is this thing about "alien flesh"? It refers to humans having sexual intercourse with angels.

Verse 6 of Jude alludes to such a story, quite obscure, in Genesis 6:1-4: "The sons of God saw the daughters of men were fair; and they took to wife such of them as they chose." (Sons of God refers to some kind of celestial beings.) Verse 7 of Jude, referring to Sodom, is meant to suggest a similar story. You will remember that the "men" who visited Sodom were really angels sent from God. So the strangeness of the intercourse here does not refer to same-sex relations but to sex between angels and humans.

Moreover, an early Jewish tradition about the story of Sodom—evident in the non-biblical Book of Jubilees 7:20-21 and 20:5-6—suggests that the *women* of Sodom wanted to have sex with the angels staying in Lot's house. If this tradition is behind the letter of Jude, it is not likely referring to same-sex acts at all—neither between humans nor between a man and an angel.

So what should we make of this text? Understandably, we might want to know more about the fascinating notion of sex with celestial beings. The movies *Cocoon*, *City of Angels* and *Galaxy Quest* successfully played on this very theme. But actually, there is not very much to tell. The whole thing is just science fiction to us. This text is irrelevant to our real-world situation and to our question about homosexual love. However, this text does provide an excellent example of how different the biblical worldview was from our own.

This text is also an excellent example of how translation can make the Bible say what it never intended. Of course, translators try to make the English rendition make sense to the reader. But sometimes what the Bible actually says just does not make sense in the 21st Century. This thing about sex with angels is a prime example. The 1989 New Revised Standard Version says Sodom "pursued unnatural lust," and the New American Bible says "practiced unnatural vice." The New Jerusalem Bible says Sodom was "equally unnatural." Now, there is nothing in the Greek text that should be translated "unnatural." In current usage "unnatural sex" refers to homogenitality. So deliberately or not, such translations foster antihomosexual sentiment. These translations are downright misleading. They are an embarrassment to modern Scripture scholarship. In this case, the vague but accurate King James translation, "going after strange flesh," deserves a tip of the hat.

Some Other Irrelevant Texts

2 Peter 2:6 mentions Sodom and Gomorrah in a list of examples of God's punishment: "by turning the cities of Sodom and Gomorrah to ashes [God] condemned them to extinction and made them an example of what is coming to the ungodly."

This verse does not say what the ungodliness of Sodom and Gomorrah was. But because the verse mentions Sodom and because they misunderstand the Story of Sodom in the first place, some people conclude the sin was homosexuality. Indeed, using this same circular reasoning, they claim that the Bible repeatedly condemns homosexuality. Anywhere Sodom is mentioned, they read homosexuality into the picture.

Today hardly anyone would hold that opinion about 2 Peter 2:6. At this point this letter is mounting its main argument, namely, that God does indeed punish the wicked, even though the return of Jesus has been long delayed. The author cites historical examples to make the point. Along with the fallen angels and the wicked of Noah's time, Sodom is listed as another instance in which God eventually punished the wicked. But this verse about Sodom makes no reference to any sexual offense. This verse does not in any way specify what the sin of Sodom was.

If a particular sin had to be specified, scholars would bet on sex with angels. For verse 4 introduces this matter when it begins, "For God did not spare the angels when they sinned." And the reference in verse 4 is back to Genesis 6:1-4, the allusion to angels having sex with human women, that was behind Jude 7, as we have already seen. Besides, scholars also believe that 2 Peter and Jude are closely related documents, for they parallel in a number of places. One such place is the passage under consideration here. 2 Peter 2:4-8 parallels Jude 5-7.

Then we are back to the weird discussion in Jude 7. The concern is sex between humans and angels. The matter is simply foreign to our worldview.

Of course, other verses in this second chapter of 2 Peter do mention sexual offenses: verse 2 notes "their licentious ways"; verse 10 notes "those who indulge their flesh in depraved lust"; verse 13 notes that the ungodly "count it a pleasure to revel in the daytime"; and verse 14 notes that "they have eyes full of adultery." However, this harangue of accusations is aimed at the false teachers against whom 2 Peter is written. It does not specify the precise sins of any particular individuals. Besides, apart from adultery, the exact nature of the licentiousness is unclear, and this fuzziness is probably deliberate. These reprimands are the standard fare of the preachers of the late First Century, who were wont to rail against excesses of desire and pleasure. These verses do not delineate the sin of Sodom. Therefore, 2 Peter 2:6 has no bearing on the discussion of homosexuality.

* * *

In a number of texts in the Hebrew Testament, the King James Bible mentions "sodomites": Deuteronomy 23:17; 1 Kings 14:24, 15:12, 22:47; 2 Kings 23:7. In this case, the King James translation gets an "F."

The Hebrew term here is *qadheshim*. Literally it means "holy" or "sacred ones." Recall from Chapter Four that the Hebrew sense of "holy" included the notion of "separated" or "set apart." Thus, as God's chosen people, Israel was to be "holy," that is, singled out and kept distinct from the Gentiles. So an equally valid translation for *qadheshim* is "devoted" or "dedicated ones." Of course, the dedication was to the Gentile gods and to service in their shrines.

Though hard evidence on the matter is almost nonexistent, scholars have suggested that this term refers to male temple prostitutes, supposedly available for ritual sex acts with both women and men. So modern translations read simply "cult prostitutes," "temple prostitutes" or "male temple prostitutes." But there is still debate among scholars whether sexual rituals really did play a part in Canaanite rites, as the Hebrew Scriptures claim.

In any case, the sin in question was not any kind of sex act. The "devoted ones" were in the service of alien gods. The sin in question was idolatry. This is clear, for example, in the Bible's comment about King Josiah. The Second Book of Kings praises him for restoring the temple, renewing the covenant with the Lord, and ridding the temple of all remnants of foreign religion. Among other things, the king "broke down the houses of the male temple prostitutes that were in the house of the Lord, where the women did weaving for [the goddess] Asherah" (2 Kings 23:7).

There is no concern about homogenital acts in these texts. Only mistranslation would suggest that.

Adam and Eve, not Adam and Steve

All the above considerations show that the Bible nowhere condemns same-sex acts in themselves. Nonetheless, the question can still be raised, But what does the Bible advocate? What is the Bible's positive teaching?

Some people choose to shift the emphasis to this other question. They assume that the Bible speaks about heterosexual relations wherever it speaks positively about sex. They conclude that, despite any interpretation of isolated texts on homogenitality, the Bible's overall attitude still does condemn same-sex acts. As one wag cutely phrased the matter, "God created Adam and Eve, not Adam and Steve." One wonders, then, who created Steve?

That argument may have emotional appeal, but it certainly is not valid. A number of considerations show this to be so.

Consider Adam and Eve and the story of creation. What was the point of those first two chapters of Genesis? The point was to present a picture of our world in its sad and sinful state and to insist that this situation was not God's doing. God created a good world of beauty and pleasure. But people misuse creation, so life becomes hard and goes sour.

Genesis is a lesson in religion, a lesson about God's way and our sin. Genesis makes its point by presenting a story, and the story involves an example. The example is the case that is by far the most common in human experience: the man, the woman, their relationship with one another, and the children they may beget. The biblical author merely presents the standard case within ancient Hebrew life. What better example would one use to make a point?

But the story is only the vehicle for conveying the religious point. The story of Adam and Eve as such is incidental to the point. Genesis is not a lesson on sexual orientation. Nothing in those two chapters suggests that heterosexuality, in contrast to homosexuality, was a concern in the author's mind. To read that modern concern into the text is simply to misuse the Bible. A similar analysis applies to all the other Bible texts about the love of woman and man for one another.

Furthermore, the Adam-and-Eve-not-Adam-and-Steve argument depends on a logical fallacy—the *ad ignorantiam* argument, argument by appeal to the unknown, argument based on assumptions about what was *not* said. The argument runs like this: since the Bible does not actively support homosexuality, it must be that the Bible condemns it. But this conclusion does not logically follow. What would follow is simply that we do not know the biblical mind on the subject.

Consider other examples where the point is much more obvious. You've heard a friend speak often and enthusiastically about his only brother, but you never heard him talk about a sister. Suppose you conclude that he has no sister or that, if he does, he certainly dislikes her. How valid is your conclusion? It is not valid at all. You know nothing about his sister nor about his special love for her. All you do know is what he happened to say about his brother.

Or again, the Bible often speaks about dogs but mentions cats only once, as roaming Babylonian temples, in Baruch 6:22. Should you conclude that the Bible is opposed to cats, and begin ridding your neighborhood of them? How valid would your position be? It is totally invalid. You know nothing about the Bible's attitude toward cats. The Bible hardly mentions them.

An endorsement of heterosexuality would imply a condemnation of homosexuality only if the two were mutually exclusive, an either-or choice. In that case, approving of one would mean condemning the other. But such a choice is not realistic. If it is real at all, it is only real in the minds of those making that argument. Obviously, then, their opinion does not depend on the Bible. On the contrary, their reading of the Bible depends on their personal opinion.

The fact that the Bible speaks often and positively about heterosexual relationships in no way implies a condemnation of homosexual ones.

This is all the more obvious since the Bible does, in fact, speak outright about homogenitality in five places, and those references intend no blanket condemnation. Moreover, in Romans Paul teaches that homogenitality is ethically neutral.

Biblical Endorsement of Homosexual Relationships?

Some scholars push the discussion to its opposite pole. Rather than merely agreeing that the Bible does not condemn homogenital acts as such, these scholars point out positive accounts of lesbian and gay relationships in the Bible.

The clearest example is the love of Jonathan and David. In a number of incidents, the First Book of Samuel suggests a deeply emotional relationship between these biblical heroes.

For example, 1 Samuel 18:1-4 recounts a striking show of affection on the part of the prince, Jonathan, toward the ruddy and handsome shepherd boy with beautiful eyes, David, newly come to court:

> The soul of Jonathan was bound to the soul of David, and Jonathan loved him as his own soul.... Jonathan made a covenant with David, because he loved him as his own soul. Jonathan stripped himself of the robe that he was wearing, and gave it to David, and his armor, and even his sword and his bow and his belt.

King Saul's angry outburst against Jonathan in 1 Samuel 20:30 is also revealing: "You son of a perverse, rebellious woman! Do I not know that you have chosen the son of Jesse [i.e., David] to your own shame, and to the shame of your mother's nakedness?" Saul insults Jonathan in two ways. First, by slandering his mother as a "perverse, rebellious woman," the outraged Saul calls his own son, Jonathan, a bastard. But second, Saul disparages Jonathan's relationship with David. The Hebrew of this verse is ambiguous and, following the Greek Septuagint translation, could also be rendered, "Do I not know that you are an intimate companion to the son of Jesse?" Then, given that the words "shame" and "nakedness" are common biblical ways of talking about sex, surely the innuendo here is sexual. It appears that Saul is deriding Jonathan's sexual liaison with David, a matter about which Saul and his whole court would have easily known. So, in contemporary terms, Saul's second insult is to call his son a faggot. At stake in this whole intrigue, of course, is rivalry over the throne of Israel.

Moreover, at their parting, Jonathan and David demonstrate an intense sorrow:

> David rose from beside the stone heap and prostrated himself with his face to the ground. He bowed three times, and they kissed each other, and wept with each other; David wept the more. Then Jonathan said to David, "Go in peace, since both of us have sworn in the name of the Lord, saying, 'The Lord shall be between me and you, and between my descendants and your descendants, forever.'" He got up and left; and Jonathan went into the city. (1 Samuel 20:41-42)

Finally, at Jonathan's death David concludes his lament with this crescendo: "I am distressed for you, my brother Jonathan; very pleasant have you been to me; your love to me was wonderful, passing the love of women" (2 Samuel 1:26).

Could the relationship between David and Jonathan have been only a deep and faithful friendship? Perhaps. But their relationship has important parallels to that of Gilgamesh and Enkidu, commonly thought to be homosexual, in the ancient Sumerian epic. That is to say, their relationship fits the model of noble military lovers, common throughout the societies of the ancient mid-East, where Israel lay. Such male-male sexual relationships were so taken for granted that they would not have had to be noted explicitly. Besides, even modern Westerners must sense something more than simple friendship in the story of David and Jonathan.

But rivalry over the throne of Israel may have been only one facet of this story. Jealousy may have been another. According to research by scholar Kamal Salibi, Saul was also in love with David (1 Samuel 16:21, 18:12, 18:28), and David was no naive and innocent shepherd boy. David was the son of an experienced and politically shrewd father (1 Samuel 17:12) and was himself scheming for power. It is possible that David actually seduced Saul. 1 Samuel 16:21 could read, "When David came to Saul and he [David] had an erection in his presence, he [Saul] loved him greatly." Later the prophet Samuel outright accused Saul of having an affair with David. Samuel protested to Saul, "Surely, thrusts in the rear are an offense" (1 Samuel 15:23). The reference is to male-male anal sex, forbidden by Jewish Law, as we have seen. And Samuel also taunted Saul, pointing out that the kingdom of Israel would pass to David, Saul's "darling" or "lover" (1 Samuel 15:27, 28:17). Moreover, Saul's daughter and Jonathan's sister, Michal, was also in love with David (1 Samuel 18:20). As is likely, in a respectable cover to this whole affair and for other reasons, Saul gave Michal to David in marriage.

You will not find this rendition of the story in any of the current biblical translations. Scholars have not yet responded to this novel and controversial reading about Saul, though detailed textual evidence does support this fascinating interpretation.

One difficulty in interpreting 1 and 2 Samuel is that they were extensively edited. Scholars are hard pressed to determine the original underlying story line. Even a casual reading of these books reveals that the story is repetitious and turns back on itself. It must be a conflation of different accounts. The original story needs to be reconstructed, and every reconstruction is a hypothesis.

Another difficulty is that written Hebrew contains no vowels; only consonants are recorded. So the written words could be spoken in a number of ways, each with a different meaning. The effect would be like coming across the English *fnd* and having to decide if the word was fend, find, fund, fond or fined. The change of one vowel makes a big difference. Thus, the standard reading of 1 Samuel 18:12, "Saul was afraid of David, because the Lord was with him (*hayah yahweh 'immow*)," could with vowel changes read "because he had been in love with him (*hayah yehaweh 'immow*)." Or 1 Samuel 16:21, that "David came to Saul and stood (*wa yya'amodh*) before him" could, with one vowel change that makes the verb reflexive, mean "had an erection (*wa yye'amodh*) before him." Or the Hebrew *uw theraphiym* in 1 Samuel 15:23 can refer to some kind of portable idol called *teraphiym*, but *wa theraphiym* means "thrusts in the rear." There is no absolute way of knowing what the correct vowels should be.

Moreover, words have different meanings. The Hebrew *re 'akha* could be cautiously translated "fellow, neighbor," but it really means something more like "special friend, lover, darling" and is in fact translated this way in the Song of Songs (1:9, 15, 2:2, etc.).

Put all these legitimate variations together and you get a very interesting reading of history. Of course, many people would prefer to stick with the traditional translations and interpretations. Why dig up all this scandal in the Bible?

The fact is that these new readings are in the text, and they do make good sense of the text. These readings square very well with the Bible in its original historical reality — very earthy, very realistic, very much involved with the messiness of human living. If substantiated, the supposed triangle among Saul, David, and Jonathan reveals that male-male sex was not so unusual in the biblical world. This affair also reveals that male-male sex, like its heterosexual counterpart, was not always used in the most ethical way.

Another case is the story of Ruth and Naomi. The Book of Ruth relates the very unusual commitment between the Jewish woman Naomi and her Moabite daughter-in-law Ruth. After the death of her husband, in contrast to the customs of the day and unlike her sister-in-law, widowed Ruth remains with Naomi. Ruth declares to Naomi, "Where you go I will go, and where you lodge I will lodge; your people shall be my people, and your God my God. Where you die, I will die—there will I be buried" (Ruth 1:16-17). This pledge of love and commitment is so impressive that the passage is often read at contemporary heterosexual marriages. Few people realize that this statement was made by one woman to another.

Unfortunately, we have very little evidence about Ruth and Naomi, so it is impossible to say whether or not they shared a sexual relationship. Nonetheless, given what we now know about the women's world in antiquity, the possibility of such a relationship is good. At that time women had their own world, significantly segregated from men, but under male domination. They often found support and affection, including sexual intimacy, among themselves. This could easily have been the case with Ruth and Naomi. As in the case of David and Jonathan, such information is not the sort of thing that the Bible is likely to report explicitly.

The Book of Daniel offers still another case. Daniel 1:9 reads, "Now God allowed Daniel to receive favor and compassion from the palace master." Another translation reads, "By the grace of God Daniel met goodwill and sympathy on the part of the chief eunuch." This text could also be translated to read that Daniel received "devoted love." Moreover, there is some serious speculation that the servants at court or the "eunuchs" in the ancient mid-East were not necessarily castrated men but rather men whose sexual interest was only for other men. For this reason they could be trusted around the harem. So some people suggest that Daniel's role in Nebuchadnezzar's court included a homosexual liaison with the palace master. The romantic connection would explain in part why Daniel's career at court advanced so favorably. And, of course, the Bible sees Daniel's success as a blessing of Divine Providence.

Were Daniel and Nebuchadnezzar's chief eunuch really lovers? Were Ruth and Naomi? Or were Jonathan and David? In the case of Jonathan and David one could impressively argue, Yes, and there is also real likelihood in the other cases. But in the end, we simply do not have the historical evidence to answer with certitude one way or the other. Here, as elsewhere in the Bible, homosexuality remains an open question. Still, the real probability of homosexual relationships in the lives of important biblical characters suggests that the Bible may be more open to same-sex love than most ever imagine.

Jesus and the Centurion's Slave Boy

We have no record of Jesus ever speaking about same-sex acts, neither in the Gospels in the Bible nor in the so-called "gnostic gospels" discovered at Nag Hammadi in 1945. This fact is telling. As Victor Furnish suggests, it implies that Jesus had nothing distinctive to say about the subject and that homosexuality was not a concern of the early church, which preserved his sayings. Without his actual statements, it is impossible to say what Jesus actually thought about homosexuality. But in this case his actions may speak louder than words, for there is evidence that Jesus encountered a male same-sex relationship during his ministry.

Both Matthew 8:5-13 and Luke 7:1-10 recount Jesus' healing the centurion's servant. Despite some interesting differences in detail, these two passages are so similar—especially when you line up the Greek texts, word for word—that scholars judge them to be based on the same written source. So we can take it that both Matthew and Luke are talking about the same situation.

Both quote the centurion saying he is not worthy to have Jesus enter his home. What is striking is this. The centurion uses two different Greek words when he speaks of his servants. He refers to the one who is sick as "my boy," *pais*. This word means boy and can also mean servant or even son. It refers to someone young and only by way of endearment to an adult. It is a word likely to refer to a slave used for male-male sex, and there is non-biblical evidence that *pais* sometimes meant male lover. In contrast, the centurion consistently refers to his other servants as *doulos*. This is the generic word for slave or servant.

Matthew always refers to the centurion's servant as *pais*. Reading Matthew, one could think the centurion was concerned about his son. But Luke, except when he is quoting the centurion, always refers to the servant as *doulos*. Luke also reveals that the boy was very valuable or dear—the Greek word is *entimos*—to the centurion. In addition, Luke notes that the centurion built the local synagogue, so the centurion must have been wealthy. It is striking that both Matthew and Luke preserve the same quote of the centurion, which marks a difference between his *pais* and his *douloi*.

What can we make of all that? First, because of Luke's emphasis, it is clear that the servant was indeed a servant (*doulos*) and not the centurion's son. And as Matthew's emphasis indicates, the servant was young (*pais*).

Second, we know that the youth was *entimos* to the centurion. This word could mean a number of things. First, perhaps the centurion paid a high price for this slave and thus did not want to lose him. But this is an unlikely reading. The centurion was wealthy and, sad to say, could easily have gone to the market to buy another slave. Second, a servant could be valuable if he were highly skilled and experienced, holding a key role in running the household. But this interpretation is also unlikely here since the boy was young. Finally, *entimos* could imply an emotional bond. This is the most likely meaning here.

Then what was the relationship between the centurion and the servant? There is no way of knowing for certain. The historical evidence is scanty. Perhaps the centurion was just a very good man and was troubled over the death of a sick slave boy. But this sentimental interpretation is modern. It is out of step with the harsh reality of life in the first-century Roman Empire. Then what would have driven a Roman centurion to go to so much trouble over a slave?

It was common that Roman householders would use their slaves for sex. It was also common for soldiers far from home to have a male sexual companion with them. The centurion and the slave boy were probably sexual partners. In this particular case, as often happened, the centurion probably fell in love with the young man. The most likely explanation of the centurion's behavior is that the young slave was the centurion's lover.

Undoubtedly, Jesus was aware of such things. He was not dumb. He knew what was going on around him. So this seems to be a case where Jesus actually encountered a loving homosexual relationship. Jesus' reaction is instructive. He commended the faith of the centurion and returned the young man to the centurion in good health.

Did Jesus think homosexuality was okay? We do not know what Jesus thought. All we know is what he said and did. In the very least he gave us a lesson on compassion: times of sickness and death are not times for preaching hellfire and damnation at people. In the era of AIDS, religious leaders could benefit from this lesson.

But the incident of the centurion's slave boy does seem to have broader implications. On the basis of the evidence, one could argue that Jesus was not disturbed by the homogenitality of his day. Moreover, Matthew and Luke did not even bother to make an issue of it. For all of them, it was faith and good will that held their interest, not sexual practices.

Some people are scandalized by the suggestion that Jesus would not have rebuked the centurion for child abuse. It is important to remember that these things had a very different meaning in Jesus' day compared with our own. To begin with, as a real human being, Jesus was very much a product of his age. We should not be surprised if he uncritically accepted key institutions of his society. For example, he was reluctant to minister to non-Jews. "It is not fair to take the children's food and throw it to the dogs," he said (Mark 7:27). He also took slavery for granted, and the master-slave relationship was a common theme in his parables. That he might likewise take for granted Roman sexual practices is not at all far fetched. Besides, childhood and youth were not as we know them today. Puberty occurred quite late, somewhere in the late teen years, there was no adolescence, and people were lucky if they lived to be 40 or so. The age difference and level of emotional maturity between a youth and an adult might not be very great. Sex with youth in the ancient world was generally not child abuse as we understand it today.

Here again the same lesson comes through that we have seen throughout this book. We need to understand things in their own historical context if we would claim to know what the Bible teaches. We need to be careful not to project our views onto Jesus and his world. The fact is that homogenital activity was common in Jesus' world. Undoubtedly, he knew about it. And we have no record of his ever making an issue of it, not even when he was face to face with it.

Nine. Summary and Conclusion

The literal approach to the Bible claims not to interpret the Bible but merely to take it for what it obviously says. The words of the Bible in modern translation are taken to mean what they mean to the reader today. On this basis the Bible is said to condemn homosexuality in a number of places.

But an historical-critical approach reads the Bible in its original historical and cultural context. This approach takes the Bible to mean, as best as can be determined, what its human authors intended to say in their own time and in their own way. Understood on its own terms, the Bible was not addressing our current questions about sexual ethics. The Bible does not condemn gay sex as we understand it today.

The sin of Sodom was inhospitality, not homosexuality. Jude condemns sex with angels, not sex between two men. Not a single Bible text indisputably refers to lesbian sex. The King James Bible's reference to "sodomites" in Deuteronomy and 1 and 2 Kings is a mistranslation. From the Bible's positive teaching about heterosexuality, there follows no valid conclusion whatsoever about homosexuality. Biblical figures like Jonathan and David, Ruth and Naomi, and Daniel may well have been involved in homogenital relationships, seen as part of God's plan. And Jesus himself said nothing at all about homosexuality, not even when face to face with a man in a gay relationship.

Only five texts in the Bible surely express an opinion about male-

male sex, Leviticus 18:22 and 20:13, Romans 1:27 and 1 Corinthians 6:9 and 1 Timothy 1:10. All these texts are concerned with something other than homogenital activity itself, and these five texts boil down to only three different issues.

First, Leviticus forbids homogenitality as a violation of the ancient Jewish aversion to the "mixing of kinds," a confusion of the idealized roles of penetrating males and penetrated females. The concern about male-male sex is impurity, an offense against the Jewish religion, not violation of the inherent nature of sex. Second, the Letter to the Romans presupposes the teaching of the Jewish Law in Leviticus, and Romans mentions male-male sex as an instance of impurity. However, Romans mentions it precisely to make the point that purity issues have no importance in Christ. Finally, in the obscure term *arsenokoitai*, if taken to refer to male same-sex acts, 1 Corinthians and 1 Timothy would condemn abuses associated with homogenital activity in the First Century: exploitation and abuse.

So the Bible takes no direct stand on the morality of homogenital acts as such nor on the morality of gay and lesbian relationships as we conceive them today. Indeed, the Bible's longest treatment of the matter, in Romans, suggests that in themselves homogenital acts have no ethical significance whatsoever. However, understood in the context of the decadent first-century Roman Empire, 1 Corinthians and 1 Timothy might suggest this lesson: abusive forms of male-male sex—and of male-female sex—must be avoided.

While the Bible makes no blanket condemnation of homogenital acts and even less of homosexuality, this does not mean that for lesbians and gay men anything goes. If they rely on the Bible for guidance and inspiration, lesbians and gay men will certainly feel bound by the core moral teachings of the Judeo-Christian tradition: be prayerful, reverence God, respect others, be loving and kind, be forgiving and merciful, be honest and be just. Work for harmony and peace. Stand up for truth. Give of yourself for all that is good, and avoid all that you know to be evil. To do that is to follow God's way. To do that is to love God with your whole heart and soul. To do that is to be a true disciple of Jesus.

Living by the Bible, gay and lesbian people will submit to those severe moral requirements—and those requirements apply also to sex and to intimate relationships.

That is all that can honestly be said about biblical teaching on homosexuality. If people would still seek to know outright if gay or lesbian sex in itself is good or evil, if homogenital acts *per se* are right or wrong, they will have to look somewhere else for an answer. For the fact of the matter is simple enough. The Bible never addresses that question. More than that, the Bible seems deliberately unconcerned about it.

133

Sources

Bailey, D. Sherwin (1955). *Homosexuality and the Western Christian Tradition*. London: Longmans, Green & Co.

A comprehensive study of the Bible texts on homosexuality, on which all further contemporary studies rely, though scholars often disagree with Bailey's conclusions. Bailey made the important, though exaggerated, argument that the sin of Sodom was inhospitality and did not involve homosexual intent.

Horner, Tom (1978). *Jonathan Loved David: Homosexuality in Biblical Times*. Philadelphia: Westminster Press.

Another comprehensive and rich study of the Bible texts on homosexuality. Horner impressively focuses on subtle and numerous allusions throughout the Bible that suggest the pervasiveness of homosexual practices in ancient mid-Eastern, including Israelite, societies. Horner suggests a highly probable homosexual relationship between Jonathan and David and a possible one between Naomi and Ruth, and also cautiously alludes to homosexual characteristics in Paul and sensitivities in Jesus.

Furnish, Victor Paul (1979). "Homosexuality." In *The Moral Teaching of Paul*. Nashville: Abingdon Press, pages 52-83.

A brief but thorough study of the Christian Testament texts on homosexuality by a specialist in Pauline ethics. Furnish concludes that Romans, 1 Corinthians and 1 Timothy do condemn homosexuality in the form known during the First Century, typified by exploitation and lust. Furnish cautions, however, that contemporary psychological understanding of sexual orientation transforms the discussion significantly, and Paul's teaching alone cannot answer today's questions about the right or wrong of homosexual behavior.

Boswell, John (1980). *Christianity, Social Tolerance and Homosexuality: Gay People in Western Europe from the Beginning of the Christian Era to the Fourteenth Century.* Chicago: University of Chicago Press.

A ground-breaking study of homosexuality from the classic era up to the high middle ages. Boswell argues that Christianity was basically indifferent to homosexuality until the late Twelfth Century and that biblical teaching was not the source of later antihomosexual Christian attitudes. This book includes a study of all the relevant biblical passages and a long appendix on *malakos* and *arsenokoitai*. On the basis of detailed word studies, Boswell argues that nowhere does the Bible condemn homosexuality *per se*. With strict attention to Pauline usage, Boswell understands *para physin* to mean "beyond the ordinary" rather than the accepted "contrary to nature." The obscure *arsenokoitai*, he insists, refers to a form of male prostitution, not to homosexuality.

Scroggs, Robin (1983). *Homosexuality in the New Testament: Contextual Background for Contemporary Debate.* Philadelphia: Fortress Press.

A thorough and careful study of the Bible and a very useful summary of the classical mindset on homosexuality. Perhaps oversimplifying, Scroggs concludes that the standard "model of homosexuality" in antiquity was pederastic, the relationship between an older man and a youth, and was often abusive, and that this is what the New Testament condemned in Romans, 1 Corinthians and 1 Timothy. Accordingly, those condemnations do not refer to what is meant by homosexuality today. Scroggs sees *arsenokoitai* as a literal Greek translation of a rabbinic term derived from Leviticus 18:22 and 20:13, and he offers references to rabbinic literature to support his case.

Wright, David F. (1984). "Homosexuals or Prostitutes: The Meaning of *ARSENOKOITAI* (1 Corinthians 6:9, 1 Timothy 1:10)." *Vigiliae Christianae* 38, 125-153.

An erudite and detailed review of *arsenokoitai* in post-biblical literature and in the earliest translations of the Christian Testament. Wright rejects Boswell's translation of *arsenokoitai* as male prostitutes and argues that it refers to "homosexuals." Wright points to the Septuagint translation of Leviticus 18:22 and 20:13 as the source of this peculiar Greek term.

Petersen, William L. (1986). "Can *ARSENOKOITAI* be Translated by 'Homosexuals'? (1 Cor. 6:9, 1 Tim. 1:10)." *Vigiliae Christianae* 40, 187-191.

Agrees with Wright's derivation of *arsenokoitai* but criticizes the translation as "homosexuals" because this term reads the twentieth-century understanding of sexual orientation into a first-century text.

Hays, Richard B. (1986). "Relations Natural and Unnatural: A Response to John Boswell's Exegesis of Romans 1." *The Journal of Religious Ethics* 14, 184-215.

Criticizes Boswell's analysis of *para physin* and argues that it does carry the Stoic sense of "contrary to the laws of nature" and that Paul saw homosexuality as a vivid image of human rejection of God's sovereignty and of the order of creation established in Genesis.

Countryman, L. William (1988). *Dirt, Greed and Sex: Sexual Ethics in the New Testament and their Implications for Today.* Philadelphia: Fortress Press.

A study of all the passages on sex in the Christian Testament. Countryman argues that biblical sexual ethics rested on two key concerns: ownership of property (greed) and purity issues (dirt). Understanding Paul's treatment of homosexual acts in Romans as a purity issue, insignificant in Christ, Countryman offers a new and important interpretation obvious in the rhetorical structure of Romans. Thus, he makes further sense of Boswell's study of the Pauline vocabulary in Romans 1. Countryman's discussion of purity issues also provides a broad context for understanding the term "abomination" and its implications in ancient Hebrew society.

Boughton, Lynne C. (1992). "Biblical Texts and Homosexuality: A Response to John Boswell." *Irish Theological Quarterly* 58, 141-153.

A broadly sweeping discussion of biblical texts on homosexuality in light of Boswell's book, though without any attention to Boswell's word study in Romans or mention of Countryman's important contribution on purity issues. Boughton unconvincingly challenges the adequacy of Boswell's argument by suggesting anachronistically that *toevah* refers to something inherently wrong, something contradicting the "fundamental nature" of a thing. Most importantly, Boughton claims that *bdelygma* was not used consistently as a translation of *toevah* to mean things only ritually forbidden. Boughton provides no specific examples or discussion on this critical point. Overall, Boughton merely shows that historical ambiguities surround this discussion.

Boswell, John (1994) *Same-sex Unions in Premodern Europe*. New York: Villard Books.

Proposes the highly controversial (and now, generally dismissed) argument that there existed Christian ceremonies for blessing same-sex relationships. Notes that the term *pais* was used to refer to the youth abducted in the ancient Cretan gay union ceremony (p. 89, p. 93 n. 198).

Furnish, Victor Paul (1994)."The Bible and Homosexuality: Reading the Texts in Context." In J. S. Siker (Editor), *Homosexuality in the Church: Both Sides of the Debate* (pages 18-35). Louisville, KY: Westminster John Knox Press.

A very useful summary on homosexuality in the Bible by a respected senior scholar. The sin of Sodom was the violation of guests. The frequent reference to "sodomites" in the King James Bible result from a mistranslation that should read "temple prostitutes." The simple concern of Leviticus is purity and has nothing to do with what is good, just, or loving behavior. There is no teaching about sexual orientation in the creation accounts of Genesis. The fact that Jesus and the Gospels never mention homosexuality indicate that Jesus had nothing distinctive to say on the topic, and that it was also evidently not a concern of the early Christians. The references in 1 Corinthians, Romans, and 1 Timothy do condemn homosexuality in the understanding of that time, namely, that same-sex activity is a deliberately chosen interest, is a temptation for everyone, is the expression of pure lust, inverts the natural roles of active and passive, and results in sterility. This condemnation merely repeats common opinion and rests on no specific theological or Christian reasoning. Thus, this condemnation presumes much than can no longer be accepted today.

Olyan, Saul M. (1994). "'And with a Male You Shall Not Lie the Lying Down of a Woman': On the Meaning and Significance of Leviticus 18:22 and 20:13." *Journal of the History of Sexuality*, Volume 5, pages 179-206.

Argues convincingly that Leviticus 18:22 and 20:13 refer only to male-male anal intercourse. Numbers 31:17, 18, 35 and Judges 21:11, 12 use the phrase *the lying down of a male*. It refers to what men offer women during sexual intercourse, and it makes a women a non-virgin. Evidently, it refers to penile penetration. The parallel phrase *the lying down of a woman* would refer to the penetrative receptivity that a woman offers a man during sexual intercourse. According to the Levitical prohibition, it is this womanly thing that a male must not get from another male. Further, in its original formulation this prohibition is addressed only to the penetrating male, not to his receptive male partner. In itself the same-sex nature of the sex act is not a matter of concern. Greek, Roman, and other Mid-Eastern societies forbade male-male sex, but the reasons regarded coercion or differences in social status. In contrast, the Levitical prohibition is universal. It applies to all males, for in the mind of the Holiness Code, male-male intercourse defiles the land. The offense was some kind of severe impurity, a mingling of two defiling agents (semen and excrement) or perhaps a mixing of kinds, namely, the violation of the boundary between maleness and femaleness, but the offense was not idolatry nor non-procreative use of sex.

Boyarin, Daniel (1995). "Are There Any Jews in 'The History of Sexuality'?" *Journal of the History of Sexuality*, Volume 5, pages 333-355.

Without dependence on Olyan, concludes convincingly that the Hebrew Scriptures did not think of sex as hetero- or homosexual but categorized sex and gender in terms of sexual penetration. Females are penetrated, and males penetrate. These roles constitute the genders and define sex. So the prohibition of Leviticus 18:22 and 20:13 applies only to male-male penetrative sex, anal intercourse. Other forms of what we would call homosexual acts, whether between women or between men, were thought of as masturbation, which the Torah does not forbid. There is a range of evidence. Fourth century rabbinical texts discuss various sexual prohibitions and treat penetrative sex, whether homo- or heterosexual, very differently from other sexual sharing. These texts allow male-female anal intercourse, but it could count as adultery, just like vaginal intercourse. For both males and females, the Bible forbids cross-dressing (Deuteronomy 22:5) and forbids sex with animals (Leviticus 18:23), yet it does not forbid sex between women, which is non-penetrative and to this extent entails no breach of the female role. Leviticus is concerned with the mixing of kinds, not with homosexuality. The parallel between the story of the Levite's concubine (Judges 19) and the story of Sodom (Genesis 19) shows that the Bible is indifferent to whether sex is hetero- or homosexual per se.

Miller, James E. (1995). "The Centurion and His Slave Boy" (unpublished manuscript).

A study of Luke 7:2-10 and Matthew 8:5-13. Argues that a most likely reading is that the servant was a catamite slave boy with whom the centurion had fallen in love. Miller does not allow that one can conclude from this incident that Jesus approved of homosexuality.

Brooten, Bernadette J. (1996). *Love Between Women: Early Christian Responses to Female Homoeroticism.* Chicago/London: The University of Chicago Press.

Presents an exhaustive discussion of the references to lesbianism in the ancient world, and there are many, especially in sources of popular culture–like formulas for erotic spells, astrological texts, medical textbooks, and a handbook on dream interpretation. There is a broad awareness of female same-sex love in the ancient world and a consistent deprecation of it, in contrast to a more tolerant attitude toward male homogenitality. These sources suggest that the ancient world did have a sense that some people are inclined toward same-sex affection. Three chapters treat Romans 1:18-32. The passage is taken as a spiraling discussion that, circling round and round, weaves a consistent argument about the evil of homogenitality. The conclusion is that Paul did condemn homogenital acts. In the popular meaning of the term, *para physin* or "unnatural" referred to what was contrary to standard cultural expectation. The focus of sexual concern in the Roman era was penetration. Women were to be penetrated, men were to penetrate, so sex between women was an anomaly and oftentimes a cause for puzzlement. Its occurrence was "unnatural," that is, it violated the social hierarchy that required women to be dependent on men. When Paul spoke of women and unnatural intercourse, according to the common usage of his day, he was referring to lesbian sex; and echoing the opinion of his day, he was condemning it. At the same time, Paul was also endorsing prevailing social standards that put women in an inferior role, for Paul was not an advocate of women's equality. If Paul did act on Galatians 3:28 as regards Jew and Gentile, he did not follow that ideal as regards the freedom of slaves nor the equality of the sexes. Given this meaning behind Paul's teaching, it should not be taken as authoritative in today's discussion of homosexuality.

Hall, B. Barbara (1996). "Homosexuality and a New Creation." In Charles Hefling (Editor), *Our Selves, Our Souls and Bodies: Sexuality and the Household of God* (pages 142-156). Cambridge, MA: Cowley Publications.

While allowing that the Old Testament texts and 1 Corinthians and 1 Timothy are irrelevant to today's discussion but that Romans 1 does condemn homosexuality in Paul's day, sees a vision in Paul's writings that would make him open to it in today's understanding. In Galatians 3:26-28 and 6:11-16 and 2 Corinthians 5:16-21, Paul radically envisages in Christ a new creation in which all polarities and social categories are superseded. Moreover, 1 Corinthians 7 shows that Paul was open to a wide variety of sexual expressions. The implication for today is that "in Christ there is no longer straight or gay."

Martin, Dale B. (1996). "*Arsenokoites* and *Malakos*: Meanings and Consequences." In R. L. Brawley (Editor), *Biblical Ethics and Homo*Index *sexuality: Listening to Scripture* (pages 117-136). Louisville, KY: Westminster John Knox Press.

Argues that those Greek words in 1 Corinthians 6:9 and 1 Timothy 1:10 simply do not refer to homosexual men; but for reasons of ideological bias more than reasons of historical criticism, in the mid-Twentieth Century focus on sexual orientation crept into the translations. The extant uses of *arsenokoitai* outside the Christian Testament relate the word to violations of justice and money matters, not specifically to homosexuality. The widely used word *malakos* should be accurately and simply translated "effeminate," but the now blatantly sexist tone of this translation makes it unacceptable. Among other things, the effeminacy in question could refer to men who groomed and adorned themselves to be sexually attractive, but such practice applied in heterosexual, as much as and more than in homosexual instances.

Hanks, Thomas (1997). "A Family Friend: Paul's Letter to the Romans as a Source of Affirmation for Queers and Their Families." In R. E. Goss and A. A. S. Strongheart (Editors), *Our Families, Our Values: Snapshots of Queer Kinship* (pages 137-149). New York/London: The Harrington Park Press.

Argues that careful attention to the kinds of communities Paul encouraged shows them to be feminist/womanist, poor and gender-bender. The people whose names Paul mentions in Romans fall into groups that do not generally fit the standard pattern of the heterosexual family. In particular, Paul was quite supportive of women.

Salibi, Kamal (1998). The Historicity of Biblical Israel: Studies in 1 & 2 Samuel. London: NABU Publications.

Presents an original and novel reconstruction of 1 & 2 Samuel in the form of seven poems that are to represent the original historical accounts behind these biblical books. Salibi brings extensive knowledge of Semitic languages to bear on the Hebrew text and concludes, among other things, that Saul and David had a sexual liaison.

Biblical Citations

Genesis
1-2 121-123
6:1-4 118, 119
19:1-11 43-44
19:28 44
34:14 93

Exodus
20:14 55, 55
22:18 55
22:25 37

Leviticus
11:3-7 57
11:9-12 57
11:14-19 58
12:2-5 57
13:13 57
15:16 57
15:19 57
18:6-18 55
18:20 55
18:22 14, 48, 51, 54, 56, 58, 59, 60, 64, 65, 92, 111, 132
18:23 55, 59
18:29 54
19:19 57
20:10 55
20:11-12 55
20:14 55
20:17 55
20:19-21 55
20:13 14, 51, 59, 92, 111
20:15-16 55
20:22 132
20:25-26 56

Numbers
5:11-31 55
19:11 57
31:17 59
31:18 59
31:35 59

Deuteronomy
5:18 55
14:3-8 57
14:9-10 57

14:11-20 58
17:20 55
17:22-23 55
22:5 59
22:11 57
22:22-27 55
23:1 55
23:11 57
23:17 120
27:21 55

Judges
19 47
21:11 59
21:12 59

Ruth
1:16-17 126

1 Samuel
15:23 125
15:27 125
16:21 124, 125
17:12 124
18:1-4 123
18:12 124
18:20 125
18:28 124
20:30 123
20:41-42 124
28:17 125

2 Samuel
1:26 124

1 Kings
14:24 120
15:12 120
22:47 120

2 Kings
23:7 120, 121

Job
36:14 93

Psalms
15:15 37
Ps 19:7 2

Proverbs
3:22 65
6:16 65
16:5 65

26:25 65
28:8 37

Song of Songs
1:9 126
1:15 126
2:2 126

Isaiah
1:10-17 49
3:9 49

Jeremiah
23:14 49

Ezekiel
14:6 65
16 65
16:48-49 48
18:12 65
18:13 37, 65.
18:17 37
18: 24 65
22:10 93
22:12 37
28:10 93

Daniel
1:9 127

Zephaniah
2:8-11 49

Wisdom of Solomon
13:1-9 84
19:13 48

Baruch
6:22 122

Jubilees
7:20-21 118
20:5-6 118

Matthew
4:7 32
5:22-29 37
5:28 71
5:32 37
6:1 70
6:6 70

8:5-13 127-130
10:5-15 48
11:8 108
15:10 70
15:18-20 70
18:38 71
19:24 31
23:27 94

Mark
7:6 71
7:27 129
10:1-13 37
10:25 31
12:42-44 71

Luke
1:34 45
4:12 32
6:18 37
8:25 31
7:1-10 127-130

John
8:32 34

Acts of the Apostles
1:28 72
10:11-15 71-72
10:14 94
10:28 94
10:34 72
11:8 94
15 71, 100

Romans
1:1 103
1:7 102
1:16 102
1:18 93
1:18-23 84
1:18-32 75, 77
1:23 93
1:24 -93-94, 95
1:24-27 88, 96
1:24-32 97
1:25 95
1:26 82, 85, 87-90, 91, 95
1:26-27 23, 77
1:27 89, 91, 98-

99, 132
1:28 83, 95, 96
1:28-32 96
1:29 7
2:1 100, 101
2:14 78
2:17 100
2:27 78
2:29 72, 101
6:9 94
7:2 81
9 101
9:5 95
9:21 90
11:13 101, 103
11:24 80, 82, 84
11:33-36 95
12:4-5 102
14:13-14 8
14:14 72, 102
14:17 112
15:5 102

1 Corinthians
4:20 112
6:9 20, 38, 105-115, 132
7 91
7:19 72
7:21-24 81
7:36 91
11:1-16 37, 81
11:5 81
11:14 78, 90
11:17-22 100
12:23 91
13:5 91
14:34-35 81
15: 24 112
15:43 91
15:50 112

2 Corinthians
5:16-17 80
6:8 90
11:21 90
12-21   94

Galatians
1:5 96

2:11-14 100
2:15 78
2:16 100
3:28 80
4:8 78
5:6 72
5:19 94
5:21 112
6:15 80

Ephesians
4:19 94
5:3-5 94
6:5-9 -36, 81

Philippians
4:20 -95

Colossians
3:5-6 94
Col 3:22-4:1 36, 81

1 Thessalonians
2:3 94
4:3-8 -94

1 Timothy
1:10 29, 38, 105-115
2:11-15 37, 81
2:9-10 37
6:1-2 36, 81

2 Timothy
2:20 90

Philemon
81

1 Peter
2:18 36, 81

2 Peter
2:2-24 120
2:6 119-120

Jude
5-7 119
6 118
7 117-119

Revelation
16:15 91

143

Index

interchangeable, 85
Daniel, 127, 131
Darwin, Charles, 11
David, and Jonathan, 123-126, 131, 135; and
    Saul, 14, 124-126, 142
death penalty, and male anal sex in Leviticus,
    51-53
demons, 12
dietary laws, 69 *See also* purity and purity laws
Dignity/USA, 17, 107
discipleship, of Jesus, 132
down-to-earth religion, and natural law, 85. *See
    also* miraculous religion
Edward II, 23
effeminacy and malakos, 108, 142; and male
    anal sex, 46, 108
Enkidu, 124
ethics, biblical, and gay sex, 19, 132-133;
    sexual, and Paul, 104, 123, 135; and biblical
    requirements, 132-133; and custom, 86; and
    Hebrew Testament and homogenital acts,
    66; and homosexuality in Letter to the
    Romans, 77, 91, 92; and Holiness Code, 56;
    and religious requirements, 55; and personal
    responsibility in Ezekiel, 65; and purity, 58,
    62-63, 66-67, 94-95, 111; and reasonable-
    ness, 40, 73; and sex, 18, 40, 126
eucharist, 33, 100
eunuchs, 127
Europe, medieval, 23
evidence, historical, 19; need for, 32
evil, 105, 132
Faith, in God, 32, 101; and love, 72
family, in Paul, 142
feminism, and Roman Empire, 82. *See also*
    women
foods, clean and unclean and Christian conflict,
    100, 102
fornication, 118
Fundamentalism, 11, 33, 34
Furnish, Victor P., 20, 127, 135, 138
Gaither, Billy Jack, 24
Galileo, 11
gay union ceremony, Cretan, 138
gays, and civil rights, 24
gender equality, and Paul, 81-82, 89, 141
Gender roles, 81; and convention, 67; and
    Leviticus, 58
Genesis, and order of creation and sexual
    orientation, 121-122, 137
Gentile(s) , 69, 72; culture, 98; and impurity,

94-95, 103; and Jews, 54, 80, 84, 89
Gibeah, 47
Gilgamesh, 124
global society, 14
Gnostic Gospels, 127
God, Creator, 12, 26, 32, 35, 40, 121; infidelity
    to, and adultery, 48; known through
    creation, 84; love of, 132; law of, 46; plan
    of, and homosexuality, 131; will of, 38;
    word of, *see* word of God; work of, 12; and
    Bible, 37; and destruction of Sodom, 44; and
    ethics, 36, 40, 82-83; and history, 38; and
    holiness, 54; and homosexuality, 18, 26; and
    human calling, 15; and human race, 27; and
    magic, 11; and miracles, 31, 32-33; and
    nature, 79, 80, 82-83, 86; and punishment,
    119; and rejection, 12; and sexual
    orientation, 26. *See also* Providence, Divine
word of God, 19, 34; and Bible, 36; and reason,
    40
Gomorrah, 44, 48, 118, 119
goodness, 32; and purity, 71
goodwill, 67. *See also* authenticity
Hall, B. Barbara, 141
Hanks, Thomas, 142
heaven, entry into, 31, 32
Hebrew Testament, 45, 51, 54, 56, 66, 88; and
    homogenital acts, 72; and Greek translation
    (Septuagint), 64, 65
Hefling, Charles, 141
heterosexuality, abuse of, 115; versus
    homosexuality, 121-122, and biblical ethics,
    121, 132; and Genesis, 137; and sexual
    ethics, 115
Hirschfeld, Magnus, 24
historical-critical method, 37-39, 40, 73, 91,
    131; meaning of, 33-34; and down-to-earth
    religion, 34-35; and inerrancy, 35; and
    Sodom story, 47. *See also* literal approach
history, 14; and change, 38; and ethics, 19
HIV, 75. *See also* AIDS
holiness, in Ancient Israel, 53-55, 120
Holiness Code, 53-55, 65; and male-male anal
    intercourse, 53-58, 139
Holy Spirit, 12, 38
homogenitality, defined, 39-40; and Bible
    openness to, 127
homophobia, 11. *See also* prejudice
homosexuality, defined, 39; deliberately
    chosen, 139; in Bible, 39-41; incidence of,
    25; in Roman Empire, pecking order, 86;

Daniel A. Helminiak, Ph.D.

Daniel Helminiak teaches psychology and spirituality at the State University of West Georgia. He holds a Ph.D. in systematic theology from Boston College and Andover Newton Theological School and a Ph.D. in educational psychology, with a specialization in human development, from The University of Texas at Austin, and he is certified as a Fellow of the American Association of Pastoral Counselors. As a psychotherapist, social scientist and theologian, he is concerned to integrate religion and psychology and thus to suggest what wholesome living means in a pluralistic and secularized world. Said otherwise, his specialization is spirituality. His areas of special interest are post-childhood development and human sexuality.

Daniel as a young priest.

Awarded a Licentiate in Sacred Theology from the Pontifical Gregorian University and ordained a Catholic priest in Rome, he initially served in a parish and subsequently pursued an educational ministry—including chaplaincy to Dignity in Boston, San Antonio, and Austin—and he has been Assistant Professor for Systematic Theology and Spirituality at Oblate School of Theology in San Antonio.

His other books are *The Same Jesus: A Contemporary Christology* (Loyola University Press, 1986), *Spiritual Development: An Interdisciplinary Study* (Loyola University Press, 1987), *The Human Core of Spirituality: Mind as Psyche and Spirit* (State University of New York Press, 1996), *Religion and the Human Sciences: An Approach via Spirituality* (State University of New York Press, 1998), *Meditation without Myth* (Crossroad Publishing Co., 2005) *Sex and the Sacred* (Haworth Press, 2006), *The Transcended Christian: Spiritual Lessons from Religious Outcasts* (Alyson Books, 2007) and *Spirituality for a Global Community: Religion, Pluralism, and Secular Society* (Rowman & Littlefield, 2008).

He has also published in numerous journals including *Anglican Theological Review, Counseling & Values, The Heythrop Journal, The International Journal for the Psychology of Religion, Journal of Sex Education and Therapy, The Journal for the Theory of Social Behavior, The Journal of Psychology and Theology, Pastoral Psychology, Soundings,* and *Spirituality Today* and is on the web at www.VisionsOfDaniel.net.

Other Books of the Spirit from Alamo Square Press

Being • Being Happy • Being Gay

Pathways to a Rewarding Life for Lesbians and Gay Men. The make-your-life-work book by Bert Herrman. "Herrman extends a compassionate and useful hand in the journey toward realizing our full human potential." —Mark Thompson, *The Advocate*. ISBN: 0-9624751-0-6/paper/$8.00

In God's Image

Christian Witness to the Need for Gay/Lesbian Equality in the Eyes of the Church by (Episcopal) Fr. Robert Warren Cromey. "Nurturing, healing...a call to action."—Malcolm Boyd. ISBN: 0-9624751-2-2/paper/$9.95

Out of the Bishop's Closet

The Daring Testimony of Faith of a Gay Mormon High Priest by Antonio A. Feliz. Fleeing the tyranny of the Church, Feliz escapes with secrets that would make Brigham Young turn pale. ISBN: 0-9624751-7-3/paper/$12.95

Lavender Reflections

Affirmations for lesbians and gay men by Eleanor Ruth Wagner with vital quotations and photographs by Victor Arimondi. "A marvelous addition to the growing library of books on affirmation"—*Lavender Lifestyle*. ISBN: 1-886360-02-2/paper/$10.95.

Two Flutes Playing

A Spiritual Journeybook for Gay Men by Andrew Ramer. "...a simple vision so steeped in age-old wisdom that it appears more contemporary than tommorrow's headlines." —Mark Thompson. ISBN: 1-886360-05-7/paper/$12.95

Out with a Passion

A United Methodist Pastor's Quest for Authenticity by Dr. Richard T. Rossiter. "Rich Rossiter's beautiful testament to the power of coming out is a potential classic of spiritual literature." —Rev. Elder Nancy Wilson, Sr. Pastor, MCC/ L.A.. ISBN: 1-886360-07-3/paper/$11.95.

Our Tribe: Queer Folk, God, Jesus and the Bible
(Millenium Edition)

Rev. Elder Nancy Wilson, senior pastor of the Metropolitan Community Church of Los Angeles, shares her touching stories as an out lesbian minister reaching out to gay men and lesbian that thought God had forsaken them. Her tales as ecumenical representative to the National Council of Churches and the World Council of Churches offer real understanding of the roots of Christian prejudice. 1-886360-10-3/paper/$14.00.

My Son, Beloved Stranger

Carrol Grady, the wife of a conservative Christian minister, learns that her son is gay and becomes a vocal advocate for gays and lesbians in the church. She tells her warm and wonderful story. 1-886360-11-1/paper/$14.95

Anti-Gay Equals Anti-God

A Minister of the Assemblies of God Explains How the Evangelical Church as Things Wrong. Dr. Samuel Behrens gives testimony of a different kind. 1-886360-12-X/paper/$14.95

To purchase copies of these books, send a check or money order for the price of each book requested plus $2.50 for the first book and $.50 for each additional book (for postage and handling) to:

Alamo Square Press
103 FR 321
Tajique, NM 87016

Checks must be drawn in U.S. currency. There is no additional cost for shipping to Canada, but readers from all other countries are required to send send $5.00 per book (for air-mail postage and handling).